Story by Jun Lennon · Art by Maki Murakami

GRAVITATION

VOICE OF TEMPTATION

HAMBURG // LONDON // LOS ANGELES // TOKYO

Gravitation: Voice of Temptation
Story by Jun Lennon
Art by Maki Murakami

Translation - Andrew Cunningham
English Adaptation - Shahan Nerses
Copy Editor - Hope Donovan
Design and Layout - Erika Terriquez
Cover Design - Anne Marie Horne
Editor - Kara Stambach

Supervising Editor - Nicole Monastirsky
Digital Imaging Manager - Chris Buford
Production Manager - Elisabeth Brizzi
Managing Editor - Lindsey Johnston
VP of Production - Ron Klamert
Editor-in-Chief - Rob Tokar
Publisher - Mike Kiley
President and C.O.O. - John Parker
C.E.O. and Chief Creative Officer - Stuart Levy

A **TOKYOPOP** Novel

TOKYOPOP Inc.
5900 Wilshire Blvd. Suite 2000
Los Angeles, CA 90036

E-mail: info@TOKYOPOP.com
Come visit us online at www.TOKYOPOP.com

ISBN: 1-59816-574-7

First TOKYOPOP printing: July 2006
10 9 8 7 6 5 4 3 2 1
Printed in the USA

CONTENTS

Tohma Seguchi

Keyboardist for Nittle Grasper and president of N-G Pro, which represents Shuichi's band. He's a tad manipulative.

Suguru Fujisaki

Keyboardist for Bad Luck. The only band member with any common sense.

Hiroshi Nakano

Guitarist for Bad Luck. He's always looking out for his partner, Shuichi. He's in love with Ayaka.

K

Bad Luck's American manager; he makes just as much trouble as Shuichi.

Sakano

Bad Luck's producer. His life is an endless succession of unbearable anxiety.

Seiren

A mysterious girl in doll-like clothing. Her inscrutable actions cause Shuichi grief.

Ryuichi Sakuma

Famed singer for Nittle Grasper. His personality totally transforms when he takes the stage.

GRAVITATION

Character Profiles

Shuichi Shindou

Lead singer for the band Bad Luck. Trying to win over his beloved, he's manages to push his way into Yuki's apartment... and heart!

Eiri Yuki

Shuichi's lover and a bestselling romance novelist. Due to a painful past, he never opens his heart to anyone, but since he met Shuichi, he's gradually begun to change.

Prologue

The warm orange glow of sunset bathed the bedroom in soft light. Shuichi heard the sound of bare feet on the tiled floor. He lazily poked his head out from the rumpled sheets. Yuki, his lover, had showered first and now stood in the doorway, drying his hair with a towel.

The older man was pale and slim, but far stronger than he looked, as Shuichi knew well. Many times Yuki had pinned him down, or wrestled him into strange positions, using his startling strength to have his wicked way with Shuichi. But it wasn't just his physical prowess that made Yuki irresistible. His lover had a beautiful, androgynous face and a jaw like a well-cut diamond. His dirty-blond hair—which Shuichi could attest was natural—felt as soft as silk, resting in choppy layers above his chiseled cheekbones. His stunning eyes were cold, piercing. Even when Shuichi stole glimpses over his shoulder, Yuki's sharp beauty made his breath catch.

"Hey, Yuki." Shuichi batted his eyelashes.

"What?" Yuki always sounded annoyed when Shuichi tried to act cute.

Shuichi even found Yuki's irritable nature adorable. If tonight weren't a special occasion, he would have pounced on the older man. But he had secret plans. Inching across the bed like a caterpillar, he looked up at Yuki with big, sad eyes.

"Will you miss me when I'm gone?"

"Naturally," Yuki said casually, turning on the hair dryer, "I won't miss you at all."

Shuichi's jaw dropped open. "How can you say that?"

"It's the truth. When you're not here, it's much quieter. I can actually get some work done."

"You love your computer more than *me?!*" Shuichi cried.

Yuki clicked off the blow dryer and turned around. His gaze was frigid. "I don't recall saying that."

Chills ran down Shuichi's spine. "Well, not in so many words . . ."

"Do you want me to lie to you?" the blond asked curtly.

Shuichi clutched his own hair and writhed in agony. *I don't understand you! You constantly send me mixed signals!*

This was going all wrong. Yuki was supposed to smile gently and say, "Don't be silly, Shuichi. You know you're number one! I'll miss you past bearing, my love!"

Why can't he follow the script? He's always so grumpy!

Shuichi fled to the bathroom. "I hate you, Yuki!" he shouted, slamming the door. He wrenched the shower tap with such force that the handle nearly broke off. Water came rushing down on his head. "C-c-c-oooold!"

"I take time out of my insanely busy schedule for you, and you call me cold in return," Yuki muttered. "You don't make any sense."

Shuichi had no trouble hearing Yuki over the noise of the shower, even through the closed door. Although Yuki had made no effort to speak loudly, Shuichi's hearing was so sensitive that he could make out every word.

I must have supersonic hearing. Or is it supersensitive? Whatever. I'm super-something. 'Course, if I keep playing gigs, I'll be super-deaf one day, but . . .

Thinking of concerts reminded him of the issue at hand.

"You know how long it'll be before we see each other again?" Shuichi whined loudly.

Shuichi was the front man for the band Bad Luck. They had finished their Tokyo performances and were about to launch a nationwide tour. It would be days before he returned. Now, Shuichi went into convulsions at the very thought of doing math, so he didn't bother to figure out exactly how long he'd be gone, but he didn't like the idea of spending even one night away from Yuki.

Shuichi shivered. He clutched his small shoulders with his thin hands. Although Shuichi was an adult, he looked like a junior high school student. (In fact, he'd once dressed up as a high school girl . . . He smiled just remembering the *look* on Yuki's face when he had appeared out of nowhere in a sailor miniskirt.) Blushing, he realized that the places where Yuki had touched him were still warm—his lover had left invisible marks on his body, proof of how deeply Yuki owned him, body and soul.

"I'm going to be so scared and lonely without you." *Why don't you understand that?* Anger and sadness welled up in Shuichi.

"Okay, sure," Yuki snapped, "I'll miss you too."

Shuichi's heart raced at those words, but in his mind's eye, he pictured Yuki secretly laughing at him.

"I can't stand it!" Shuichi shouted, banging his head against the shower tile. *You drive me crazy!*

Why do you make me love you so damned much?!
"You're a novelist! You should know how to say something more . . . more . . . semantic at a time like this!"

"You mean 'romantic'?"

"Don't start with the red pen! Say something sweet!" Shuichi howled. "Tell me something to comfort me during those lonely nights in Osaka!"

"All right. Let me say this . . ."

Shuichi turned the shower off, breathless with anticipation. It was so silent that he could hear the water dripping off his body.

"Don't project your anxiety onto me," Yuki said. "You're stressed because this is your first national tour."

Yuki's words went straight to his heart. He staggered back against the wall and closed his eyes. Something in him snapped.

"Stress?! I have no stress! I am perfectly calm!" Shuichi bolted out of the bathroom, dragging the showerhead after him, holding it like a mike. He quickly launched into a flamboyant, buck-naked performance that would have made Bad Luck infamous if it were on TV. "Hey, everyone having fun yet? I'm Shuichi Shindou, and this is Bad Luck! Bring on the tour! I'll sing my heart out for all of you! Clap your hands, everybody, because it all starts here!"

"Or *ends* here," Yuki said sarcastically. "If you freak out this much over one silly tour, your career is as good as finished."

"It is not! It's not only me—Hiro and Suguru are raring to go, too! We're all just really excited. And Nittle Grasper is gonna help us start things off by making a guest appearance at the Osaka show!"

Fully dressed and hair now dry, Yuki sat on the edge of the bed. He puffed on a cigarette and raked his eyes over Shuichi's naked body. His gaze was still cold, but there was a tender smile on his handsome face. Shuichi's anger dissolved.

The older man blew smoke at him. "See? You won't be lonely. You've got your friends."

"Yuki!" *So you are worried about me after all. I'm so sorry I ever doubted your love!* Tears spilled down his cheeks. Through the blur, the blond looked like he was crowned with a halo. Shuichi sighed.

"You're right," he admitted. "I *am* stressed. I'm worried about the clubs and the audiences and everything else."

"I'm worried about that myself," Yuki confessed.

It was very likely that Shuichi would get carried away when he was on stage and yell, "I love you, Yuki!" or something equally stupid. If he did, it wouldn't be the first time—Shuichi wasn't known for his discretion. Thanks to his impulsive personality, his relationship with Yuki was already all over the tabloids.

"I mean," Shuichi said, "what if crazy fangirls drag me off the stage? I'm so worried about that, I can barely sleep!"

Yuki ground his teeth and flung a pair of pajamas at Shuichi. "Hurry up and get dressed. You're being ridiculous."

Shuichi tossed the clothes aside and lay down next to Yuki. He nuzzled the older man's chest. "You don't like looking at my naked body? Come on, Yuki," he smiled seductively, "let's make up for all the fun I'm gonna miss."

He nipped at Yuki's shoulder.

Shuichi's secret plan was to spend the entire evening flirting, getting his lover all hot and bothered, and then . . . He'd certainly rather do *that* than think about his separation anxiety. He knew that Yuki's love would give him all the strength he needed for the tour.

The older man slipped his arm around Shuichi's shoulders, leaned over, and whispered into his ear, "Sorry, gotta go. I already have a date."

Shuichi reeled. "Tonight? Wait—*date?* With who?"

Yuki grinned, pure bliss flashing across his beautiful face. "My poor, lonely keyboard. It's been waiting for my skilled fingers for far too long." Yuki nodded toward his study, where the laptop rested on his desk.

"But I'm leaving tomorrow!"

"Yes, I know," Yuki said cheerfully. "You'll need plenty of rest. It's such hard work being a rock star. You should take better care of yourself. Besides, my deadline is tomorrow. I'll be up all night."

"But, Yuki," Shuichi cried. Yuki was already headed toward his study door, and Shuichi could only stare after him. "You *always* have a deadline," he muttered.

"What can I say? I'm a slow writer." Yuki shrugged.

Shuichi nodded. "I know. And I'm glad you're so famous and have millions of fans that care if your book is late, but . . ."

Yuki just grunted, booting up the computer.

Shuichi attempted to distract his lover by dancing seductively, but Yuki just put his glasses on and sat down at his desk. He left the door open, as if it was too much trouble to close it.

Shuichi clung to doorframe like an abandoned child, peering in. There was something spellbinding about the irritated way Yuki pounded at the keys.

He always cuts me off and starts working, but . . .

"Hey," Shuichi said. "Just one last thing?"

The only answer was the sound of tapping keys.

"You have any time after this deadline?" Shuichi asked.

"I've got another one a week from tomorrow."

"Oh, seriously? Sweet! That's our last day in Hiroshima, and we've got some time off before we play in Osaka."

If K, his manager, had heard Shuichi just then, he probably would've poked him with a gun and demanded to know what the hell he meant by "time off." But Shuichi's head was spinning with the notion of a sex-filled vacation, and there was no room left to think about such trivial details.

"So, when that next deadline's over, maybe we could visit your folks?"

"Dream on," Yuki growled.

"Doesn't the thought of Kyoto make you want to jump on the next bullet train? Cherry blossoms, ancient temples, delicious pastries . . ."

"You sound like a travel agent," Yuki rebuked, scribbling a note on a piece of paper.

"Please, please, *please* come meet me! Hiro and Ayaka have a date, too."

"They have a long-distance relationship," Yuki said. "Let them have their fun."

"They still see more of each other than we do! I want to have a romantic date in Osaka or Kyoto or even Kobe!" he screamed.

Instead of answering, Yuki balled up a piece of paper and threw it over his shoulder. It sailed right into Shuichi's open mouth.

"Yuck!" He spit it out.

"I see you right here every day. Why should I go to all that trouble?" Yuki asked.

"You know why." Shuichi grinned.

Yuki's editors knew he had a habit of vanishing before his deadlines. But he had stopped doing that since he'd started dating Shuichi, preferring instead to spend most of his time at home. His editors were all extremely thankful to Shuichi for the change.

"You're sulking because I'm leaving you here all alone, aren't you?" Shuichi asked. *Yuki wants to tell me to stay, but he can't be honest with himself. No matter what he says, I know he must be anxious to have me back.* A wave of love washed over Shuichi like a tsunami.

"You sure are so cute sometimes," Shuichi said. "You slay me."

Yuki's hands moved off the keyboard and grabbed a hefty dictionary. "I will slay you, literally, if that's what it'll take to get you to go to sleep."

Still, Shuichi felt optimistic. "If you don't want to come see me, that's fine. I'll work my butt off and find some way to come back! I promise!"

Without waiting for an answer, Shuichi danced out of the room, composing a strange little tune on the spot. "Yuki has a *dead*line . . . Me, I'm feeling *just* fine. We'll spend that time to*gether*. Our love will last for*evaaaaaaah*—"

THUMP! The dictionary hit him on the back of the head, and he toppled over. The study door slammed shut and, seconds later, the sound of typing resumed.

Struggling to retain consciousness, Shuichi felt that even though his secret plans for nookie were thwarted, at least now he would be able to concentrate on work.

"Just you wait, Yuki. When I come home, you won't be able to pry me off of you with a crowbar!"

The heart is made of fire.
You can't command the flames.
Burning, twined together.
Love's a force, untamed.

It's Gravitation . . .

Track One:
Where Has the Love Express Gone?

"I'm counting on you, Nozomi!" Shuichi said, slapping the seat in front of him like a coach might encourage a batter who needed to hit a home run to win the World Series. But Shuichi wasn't talking to a *person*. He was talking to the bullet train that had begun to slide out of the station.

"Faster than the speed of light! Take me back to Tokyo, dear Nozomi!" Shuichi slapped the chair again enthusiastically.

"I think the speed of light's a bit too much to ask for," Hiro said, not bothering to turn around. He sat right in front of Shuichi.

Hiroshi Nakano had helped get Bad Luck off the ground when he and Shuichi were still in high school. He played the guitar, and, unlike Shuichi, he was clearheaded and mature. Suguru Fujisaki, the keyboardist, was also on the train, sitting farther away with the rest of the band's entourage. Everyone was doing their best to ignore Shuichi's outburst.

"Even the Concorde can barely break the sound barrier," Hiro added.

"I just wanna make sure we're not late for our live radio appearance."

Hiro knew this was a lie. When Shuichi had said he wanted to slip away between the Hiroshima and Osaka performances, both his manager and producer had instantly rejected the idea.

Tohma Seguchi, the president of Bad Luck's record label, knew why Shuichi wanted to go home. He had done his best to make Shuichi's trip back impossible.

Tohma had scheduled the band to appear on a radio show in Tokyo that evening. It would be a late night broadcast, and they would have to catch the first train to Osaka the next day.

"Yeah, right," Hiro said. "The radio show. You can fool yourself, but you can't fool me. You just want to see Yuki again." He knew very well that Shuichi couldn't stand to be apart from the novelist for long without succumbing to severe depression.

"Don't even say his name!" Shuichi kicked Hiro's seat. "I'm trying really, really hard not to say it, so you can't either!" Shuichi leaned forward over the back of the seat and shook his partner's shoulders.

"You're a mess." Hiro laughed, combing his fingers through his long hair.

"Yeah, the symptoms are getting worse. For a second yesterday, I thought everyone in the entire audience looked like Yuki. I nearly dove off the stage. It was pretty close. I mean, I thought I was safe when I was singing, but . . ."

"I think you've done pretty good, considering. But the tour's barely started."

"I know! What am I going to do?" Shuichi wailed, clenching his fists. He hopped up and stood in the aisle, shuddering, agonized. "I can't wait any longer! My body can't survive without Yuki. I need him all through the night!"

Just as Shuichi was about to get too personal, the train slammed on its brakes. He fell flat on his face. The floor was covered in thick carpeting, but he fell so hard that when he got up there was a thin trail of blood streaming out his nose.

"Cruel fate!" He shook his fist in the direction of the conductor. "An entertainer's face is his livelihood! It's his life!"

"Oh, no," a soft voice said. "Are you okay?"

Shuichi turned to see a young girl surrounded by an enormous explosion of frills and lace. "Oh, hello, Lolita."

"What?" The innocent-looking bundle of Victorian frippery cocked her head to one side.

"Oh, forget it! I'm okay, thanks," Shuichi cried, leaping to his feet forcefully. He finally got a good look at her. It was like she'd just stepped out of a time machine. She wore a knee-high skirt over a petticoat that had a million layers of crinoline. And her hair was done up, too, in big, dramatic curls that were tied with frilly ribbons. She looked like a giant French doll that had come to life in a science experiment gone horribly wrong.

"Wow," Shuichi mumbled, overwhelmed by the girl's strange beauty.

"Are you Shuichi Shindou from Bad Luck?" she asked.

"Uh, yes. I am."

"Um . . ." she hung her head, barely able to get the words out, "I wanted to meet you. So I got on your train. Could you, um . . . sign this for me?"

"Sure," Shuichi said.

Now that Bad Luck's album was selling well, the band was constantly chased by fans. Packs of girls would materialize out of nowhere and run after them like hungry wolves. But this was the first time a fan had followed Bad Luck onto a train.

"This is all I have," the doll-girl said, shifting around nervously, unable to meet his eyes, "but could you sign it?"

"Sure! I'll sign anything for a fan!" he said cheerfully, taking the pen and white thing she handed him.

The texture of the white cloth made him stiffen. It felt so soft. It had lace on its edges. *It feels like a stocking. And it's still warm!*

"You want mè to sign *this?*" Shuichi gulped.

"Yes. I want to be with you always," the girl announced, her petticoat crinkling loudly. "I want to feel you *close.* Is that weird?"

"No, no, um . . . not at all. I'm, uh, honored!" He laughed nervously.

It took some courage to hand something like this over to another person. Out of respect for her resolve, Shuichi went along with it. "Hiro, hold this end?"

"Uh, sure."

Both of them blushed as they unfurled the recently worn cloth.

"Right here," she said. She pointed her gloved finger to the bottom of the cloth.

Shuichi signed his autograph in a big, manly flourish. Unable to endure the silence, he began babbling. "Gosh, this just makes me wanna take a sniff! There's some sort of floral scent." (Blood still running down his nose, he looked like a raving fetishist to the other train riders.)

"Yes, it's scented with rose water," she said, completely unperturbed.

"Speaking of roses, I hear there's a restaurant in Osaka that puts rose petals and pork on their pizzas," Shuichi gabbed on. "Gotta try that while we're there."

The girl just stared at Shuichi with admiration. Shuichi began to feel desperate.

"What's your name?" Hiro asked the girl, trying to give Shuichi a break. He always kept a close eye on his partner.

"Seiren," she said.

"S-e-i-r-e-n? That's an unusual name."

Shuichi returned the stocking and watched as the girl hiked up the hem of her lace-fringed dress.

"Here," Hiro said coolly, offering his hand. As if it were only natural, Seiren held it and raised her foot. With a ballerina's poise, she put on the stocking Shuichi had signed.

"Thank you very much."

27

"No, not at all! I'm glad you like it," Shuichi said, nodding vigorously.

Without warning, she reached for his head and pulled out a few hairs.

"Ow! What'd you do that for?" he yelped, rubbing his scalp.

Seiren placed the hairs in the center of a lace handkerchief and folded it carefully around them.

"What the hell?!" Shuichi yelled.

"Don't you think that's going a bit too far?" Hiro said to the girl, still smiling.

"I shall make good use of them," Seiren said, smiling back at Hiro. "Goodbye."

"My *hair!*" Shuichi wailed.

Ignoring him, the girl calmly returned to her seat. Shuichi kept standing for a while, lost in thought. *Something doesn't fit.* He stared suspiciously at the doll-girl. She was just sitting there, calmly absorbed in a book, as if nothing had happened.

"Why my hair?" Shuichi mumbled.

"Don't worry about it," Hiro said. "Your fans are all a little crazy."

"They are not!"

"Birds of a feather flock together."

"I don't have any feathers, silly," Shuichi grumbled.

Hiro sighed. "Normal people don't want the name of the man they love written on their foot so that they can step on it all day long."

"I'd rather *die* than do that!" For Shuichi, Yuki's name was sacred; it was the most beautiful word in existence. "You think that girl is *really* a fan?"

Hiro shrugged. "How should I know?"

"Well, I could swear she never actually said that she was."

"That's strange," Hiro said.

"Don't underestimate your fans, Shuichi," Suguru suddenly whispered, butting in on their conversation.

Suguru had only recently graduated from high school, but he was by far the smartest and most mature member of the group. He was especially adept at pretending to be a complete stranger whenever Shuichi did something stupid.

"She gave off the same sort of vibe you do, Shuichi. In other words, she's not even *close* to normal."

"Is that what you think of me? Aw, shucks, you're making me blush."

"Shuichi." Hiro sighed. "How could you take that as a compliment?"

"Forget it, Hiro," Suguru said. "Sarcasm is lost on him."

A thin man wearing a suit and tie came wobbling down the aisle carrying a pile of fast food lunches. It was Bad Luck's producer, Sakano.

"Poor me. I was in the middle of buying these lunches at the train station when the *shinkansen* started to leave," he said, removing his glasses and wiping the sweat from his brow. "Luckily, K was with me. He held the station guards at gunpoint until they stopped the train and let us board."

"Uh huh," Shuichi said, grabbing his lunch from Sakano. "Hey, wait! That means it was *your* fault I fell on my face!" he yelled at his manager, K, who was walking up behind Sakano.

"Don't be angry, Shuichi!" The blond-haired, blue-eyed American grinned pleasantly—a jarring contrast to the nasty rifle slung over his shoulder. K was in flagrant violation of the gun control laws, but he always got away with it. He drew his beloved magnum from his side and said, "Our mission was fraught with danger, but after an epic struggle, we were able to acquire your lunches. Eat every bite, or I'll be forced to shoot you."

"Put that thing away!" Shuichi cried. "This is Japan. We're a peaceful nation!"

Suddenly, there was a loud, hollow explosion. A cloud of white, floury smoke burst forth from the car door. It puffed and spread, quickly filling the compartment with the harmless kind of haze used in rock concerts and theater productions.

At the source of the blast lay a pitiable man. He wore a suit; his tie flapped up over his head. The automatic door thumped open and closed against his side.

"Got one!" K said triumphantly.

Shuichi had a sinking feeling in his gut. "What do you mean?"

"I set a smoke bomb up at the door. Whenever someone tries to pass through without a chip that has the coded signal, it explodes."

Shuichi frowned. "What? You mean, it was just my imagination that my fans' manners had improved? It was actually just because no one could get through your crazy smoke bombs?"

"That's right, baby. But really, no need to thank me." K beamed confidently. "It's my job."

"You're not getting any thanks!" Shuichi looked ready to burst into tears.

Hiro and Suguru glanced at each other and then plastered fake smiles on their faces.

"We don't have any special signal-broadcasting chips implanted in *us*, do we?" Suguru asked.

"I wish I could say for sure," K said, scratching his chin.

Suguru hung his head and heaved out a great puff of air.

"We shouldn't sigh so often, Suguru," Hiro said. "They say it chases away happiness."

"No matter how much we suffer, Shuichi and K are *always* happy," Suguru said.

"Let's go help their greatest victim," Hiro suggested. They turned toward Sakano, who had fainted from shock when the bomb went off. "Hey, man, are you okay?"

"I know sometimes it's all too much to bear," Suguru tried to comfort him, "but you really need to start getting used to this sort of thing."

"Huh?" Sakano regained consciousness. He was familiar with K's antics by now, but he still felt he had to say something. "K! Popularity is everything in this business! You have to think more carefully before doing anything dangerous—especially if it might *kill* one of our fans!"

K nodded cheerfully. "Right. Sure."

"Okay, now, everyone remain calm," Sakano said shakily. "First we have to do something about *him.*" He pointed toward the man who lay in the doorway; the door was still opening and closing on his side.

"Destroy the evidence," K suggested, fingering his magnum.

Ignoring him, Sakano went over to the man. "I'm so sorry! Are you hurt? That, um, *device* makes a loud noise and startles everyone, but really it can't actually injure or kill you." Sakano smiled nervously. "You're just in shock. Here." He held out a can of hot tea to the groaning victim. "This should help your nerves."

"This is no time to be drinking tea!" Shuichi said, snatching the can out of Sakano's hand.

"But what else can I do?" Sakano asked. His lower lip trembled and then he collapsed into an avalanche of sobs.

While Shuichi drank the tea, Hiro and Suguru helped the victim up and took him to his seat.

"Sorry for all the fuss," Hiro said calmly, smiling to the passengers who were unlucky enough to be seated near them. He returned to his seat, leaned over the back, and whispered, "Shuichi, she's definitely not normal."

"Who?"

"Doll-girl. Your so-called fan. She's got headphones on while she's reading a book. And, like, she didn't even notice the explosion."

"Seriously?"

"I think that just makes her a typical Bad Luck fan," Suguru said with resignation.

Shuichi watched K as he got busy setting up another smoke bomb at the door. *K's always doing this kind of crap. Maybe our groupies just think this is the way things are supposed to be with popular bands.*

"Come to think of it," Shuichi said, "Yuki's not surprised anymore when K drags me away at gunpoint. All he does is let me give him a goodbye kiss." A lusty smile appeared on Shuichi's lips. These kisses were always followed by a punch or a kick out the door, but even the mild pain seemed attractive now.

"Yuki! I'll be home soon!" Shuichi yelled.

Hiro and Suguru stared at him.

"Don't look at me like that," Shuichi said. "You know I belong to Yuki!"

Both waved their hands at Shuichi. He was delusional if he thought they wanted to jump his bones.

"You should call and tell him that," Hiro said.

"You haven't called him today?" Suguru added. "That sounds like a catastrophe in the making to me."

Shuichi glared. "Have you never heard of something called true love? Yuki had a deadline yesterday. He's probably asleep right now, so because I love him, I'm not letting myself call."

"Wow, that *is* impressive," Suguru said, unfazed. "But definitely a bad omen."

Hiro suppressed a smile. "Yuki doesn't sleep for three days before a deadline, right? Then he probably *is* asleep."

"Exactly. So when I get home . . ." Shuichi began swirling his finger on Hiro's head, looping his long hair like noodles around chopsticks.

"Right into bed!" Suguru blurted out, then turned slightly green. "Oh man, I said that out loud!"

"Uh-huh." Hiro smirked.

"Oh. Okay. Um . . . Yeah . . . I'm going to sleep now," Suguru said.

"I'm sure he's waiting for me!" Shuichi wriggled with anticipation.

It had been so many days since they'd been together . . . *I'll cling to Yuki all night long.* His mind emptied of everything but desire.

"But maybe I *should* call," Shuichi said. "Just to hear his voice . . . No, no, I can't! But I want to. But time apart makes our love grow. But maybe I should call . . . No, I shouldn't . . . But . . . !" Shuichi started yanking out his hair.

"Shuichi, please!" Hiro's smile faltered for a second. "Just call him!"

"Oh, Yuki! You drive me crazy! I love you!"

The express train hurtled out of Tokyo, almost glowing with the fire of Shuichi's passion.

Just a few hours later, Bad Luck was in the studio of the most popular Tokyo radio station. Cheery music played in the background as the live broadcast began. Hiro, Suguru, and Shuichi wore headsets and beamed with nervous excitement as they sat around a table rigged with microphones.

"And so, at last, Bad Luck has started their first national tour," the radio hostess said, not wasting any time.

"Yeah!" Shuichi shouted. "We've started!"

"We've done our share of concerts," Hiro said, "but the response is a little different in each city, and we're just so happy that we've been welcomed all over the country."

"Totally! We're *so* touched!" Shuichi burst out again.

"Exactly," Suguru added. "It's a great feeling to be met with open arms by fans across the nation, and we're looking forward to playing Osaka tomorrow. We've changed the set list a little for that show, and it should make the concert even better."

"Hooray! New set list! We're gonna rock!" Shuichi jumped up and down in his seat.

"That's good to hear," the hostess managed, trying desperately to ignore Shuichi's childish antics. "I'm sure everyone's looking forward to it."

"We're more than looking forward to it!" Shuichi cried. " 'Good things come to those who date! If you love your children, then make them wear socks!' That's what I'm talking about!"

The hostess started to panic, but Hiro and Suguru were so used to Shuichi that they just smiled and tried their best to move on.

"Shuichi," Suguru said, "maybe you're getting a bit too worked up?"

"Shuichi puts a hundred percent into everything he ever does, folks," Hiro said gently into the microphone.

"Aren't you all enjoying yourselves?" Shuichi asked. "I've never been happier in my entire life!"

Even if he hadn't announced it, it was painfully obvious. He radiated bliss because when this job was finished he could go home and see Yuki. Just sitting next to him put people in danger of being burned by his shining aura. In fact, his joy was so strong that it had almost broadcast itself through the airwaves to every corner of the nation.

"Shuichi, if you overdo it tonight, you'll be too tired to sing tomorrow," Hiro warned, but his words couldn't penetrate Shuichi's force field of ecstasy.

"Whatever, Hiro. Don't worry about me. The one you really should worry about is Yu—"

"Shuichi!" Suguru shouted, realizing his bandmate was about to blurt out Yuki's name. "We've all heard how worked up Osaka audiences get, so please save some of that energy for them!"

"Oh, yeah! Osakans are the party animals of Japan! We'll dance all night! Oh powerful, burning love! Love, love, love!" He began to hop around.

Frightened by Shuichi's sudden monkey dance, the hostess quickly introduced the next song, Bad Luck's debut single, before leaving the booth.

Through the glass, they could see her gesturing angrily at the program director.

"I think I'm beginning to see why we're hardly ever invited to respectable talk shows," Suguru said.

"Stop complaining," Hiro said. "These days legitimate artists and actors all want to get on variety shows. There's no shame that we started there! I think we're pretty lucky."

"Do you really believe that?" Suguru asked, his eyes widening.

Hiro simply smiled.

The hostess came back into the studio before the song finished. "Next, we're going to have you give the listeners some advice on their troubles. Try to think of helpful responses," she told them. She handed Shuichi a postcard that a listener had sent in and then smiled brightly, her gloom gone.

"This!" Suguru whispered, pained. "This is what our band lacks!"

"The professionalism to handle any situation with ease?" Hiro murmured, glancing at Shuichi.

As Shuichi read the postcard intently, his expression changed completely. Hiro knew full well that this was Shuichi's most dangerous expression—there was no telling what he'd come out with next.

"If he'd been an uptight, responsible guy," Hiro said to Suguru, "I'd never have played with him."

"Huh?"

"No matter how good you are, if you're always the same—if you're *just* consistent—it gets very boring, very fast," Hiro explained.

Suguru looked annoyed. "I think consistency and being boring would be a worthy goal for *us!*"

Hiro shrugged. "Maybe I'm just attracted to unpredictable people because I'm so ordinary myself."

"Attracted!" Suguru said in disbelief. "I feel like the brakes went out, and I've been flung off the motorcycle, and I'm about to suffer multiple compound fractures."

Suguru sat muttering to himself unhappily. He had been feeling unbalanced for a while now. Like he was becoming someone else, as if Shuichi's weirdness was contagious. He felt like his personality had been put through the grinder, and it had come out on the other side unrecognizable.

If he hadn't met someone with Shuichi's passion and power, he would never have been able to change. He would still be that know-it-all, honor roll student whom everyone despised. Suguru wasn't alone; thousands of fans had been changed by Shuichi's unbridled energy.

Having read the postcard carefully, Shuichi handed it back to the hostess just as the song ended. The advice segment of the show began with a jingle so cheery it bordered on being sarcastic.

"Good evening, everyone," the hostess said.

"Good evening!" the guys said happily.

"Here's our first letter: 'I'm a great fan of Bad Luck. I'm an administrative assistant, and I'm twenty-three. I've been seeing my boyfriend since college, and we both got jobs at the companies we'd hoped for.' "

"Not so easy these days," Suguru said.

"Congratulations," Hiro added.

Shuichi was indignant. "How can you be so flippant?" he asked his bandmates. "We're giving advice on love here! Love! Bite your tongues!"

POW! BAM! Shuichi mercilessly punched both of them. They were sent flying off their chairs.

Reeling from shock, the hostess forced herself to read on as if nothing had happened.

" 'Recently, though, he seems to be very busy at work and has had to cancel a number of our dates. I'm enjoying my job a lot now that I'm used to it, and I always leave on time. But all that awaits me after work is a message on my answering machine, or worse, a text message on my mobile. Even when we do meet, we just end up arguing. I don't know what to do. Please help me!' And it's signed, 'Oh Dear.' "

The hostess turned to the band. "So this is our listener's problem. Bad Luck, what do you think? All of you are very busy with work as well, so perhaps you could give her some good advice?"

The listener's problem was almost identical to Shuichi's own difficulties. His clenched fist shook. His face turned bright red. He seemed to be straining against something.

Hiro and Suguru could tell Shuichi was on the verge of saying something that would get them in trouble. They leapt back on their chairs and started yammering.

"Wow, that's a tough problem!" Hiro said.

Suguru cleared his throat. "I'm a little too young to worry about balancing work and love."

Hiro kept his answers deliberately vague, while Suguru tried to be constructive.

"Men generally don't think about love until they've established themselves at work."

Hiro nodded. "I agree. Maybe you should be patient 'til he's more settled?"

"So you think I'm right to suggest work is important to men?" Suguru asked.

"Both men and women think their jobs are important, but the actual degree is probably different for different people."

Suguru nodded to the hostess. "I think it's best if you talk this out calmly. Try to understand each other's feelings." He sighed. "All we can think about these days is our tour, so it's pretty hard for us to give you good advice. Sorry!"

"And none of us have girlfriends," Hiro added awkwardly. (He himself had barely managed to get beyond holding hands with Ayaka.) And while Suguru would probably keep it hidden if he had a girlfriend, at the moment he *didn't* have one. Hiro had hoped to ease safely past the topic with his last comment, but the hostess pressed on.

"Oh?" she said. "But I heard that Shuichi has a lover?"

"Ah!" both Hiro and Suguru shrieked with enough force to knock the microphones out. They had almost wormed their way out of it, but the hostess had to go and step on a land mine.

"I've heard," she continued, "that his lover is the renowned romance writer Eiri Yuki?"

"Silence!" Shuichi roared. "It's always work, work, work! I love you more than work, don't I? Can you go out to dinner with your job?"

"Without a job, you can't eat at all," she pointed out.

"Can you be happy with only your job, lady?"

"Shuichi!" his partners tried to cover his mouth with their hands, but it didn't work.

"Can you kiss your job? You can't, can you?" He stared at the woman.

"Shuichi, stop!" Sakano screamed, hands clinging to the glass outside the studio as he slowly collapsed.

"Ha ha ha! Sorry about that outburst, everyone!" Hiro said. "Shuichi tends to get a little too emotional."

"I do apologize to the person who sent in the postcard," Suguru said. "But all I can say is that you picked the wrong people to ask for advice."

"What do you mean?" Shuichi interrupted. "There's no one on Earth better suited to answering this question than me!"

By now, Shuichi's yearning for Yuki had reached Herculean proportions. He was past the point of no return.

"I know just how you feel, Akko!" Shuichi said.

"No, Shuichi! That's her *real* name!" the hostess blurted out.

"If you hadn't said so, no one would've noticed," Hiro pointed out.

"You're right, Hiro," Suguru agreed.

The hostess froze. Her nerves were shot. Her pupils were dilated, and she stared blankly ahead.

Meanwhile, Shuichi grew even more passionate, swinging his fist around like a melodramatic *enka* crooner. "This is no time to worry about *that!* Akko, unless something changes, we'll just end up waiting for the rest of our lives! And they won't ever notice!"

"Interesting point," the hostess mumbled.

"I mean, why did they ever fall in love with us in the first place?"

"You should never take being loved for granted, is what you mean?" Hiro said, trying to follow along with him.

"Of course you should!" Shuichi said. "It's a huge problem if you can't trust your love!"

"Make up your mind!" Suguru said. Both he and Hiro had realized that the conversation was veering too close toward Shuichi's personal problems. They tried to get things back on track.

"Calm down, Shuichi!" Hiro said. "It's not going to help her if you melt down!"

"Who cares?" Shuichi moaned.

"I'm sure your boyfriend feels bad about having to work all the time, so maybe if you communicate, if you just work together . . ." Hiro tried.

Shuichi nodded. "Yeah, with men, actions speak louder than words, but they do have feelings, too. There are tons of strong and silent types with big hearts."

It seemed to be working. Shuichi was calming down. He was still breathing hard enough to knock the foam off a beer, but at least he'd stopped ranting.

"Yeah. Maybe," Shuichi murmured to himself, suddenly dreamy. It was like someone had flipped a switch inside him. "Oh, the sight of you at work is so exquisite, so magnificent, so breathtaking! I want to put it in the treasure chest of my heart and throw away the key!" Shuichi radiated bliss even more powerfully than before. His face was overcome with a lusty expression and he looked ready to violate broadcast regulations. "It's so *hot* when you're working! I'm not complaining! Do what you have to!"

His complete reversal left the others in the dust. Apparently oblivious, he raced onward. "You always throw yourself into work, body and soul, like there's no space left for you to think about me. I think about you twenty-four seven. It's not like it doesn't hurt." Shuichi's feelings rushed out on the strong current of his voice, filling the night air, riding on radio waves and spreading across all of Japan.

"But still, I'm always here for you!" Shuichi continued. "I'm open at your convenience, any time you need me. Come right in. I *never* close!"

Suguru and Hiro quickly tried to translate his babbling into something meaningful for the audience. They feared that if they didn't, and if Shuichi kept talking, they'd all get into a lot of trouble.

"So if she were to *see* her boyfriend working," Suguru struggled, "she would fall in love with him again?"

"While he's stuck working overtime," Hiro said, "she could bring him dinner at work?"

"I've brought some goodies!" Shuichi babbled uncontrollably. "I grabbed some cheesecake—no, cream puffs, now your mouth and pop one in. Or I'll cut one in half for us to share, because then it will taste better. Or better yet . . ."

Hiro struggled to keep up. "It would be one thing if you didn't love him anymore, but you're angry because you still do, right, Akko? You'd be perfectly happy if you could be by his side all the time." He sounded cheerful, but the pain of being away from Ayaka began to temper his voice. "It's important to value the time you *do* have together."

"But if you've already reached the stage where all you can do is fight every time you see each other," Suguru said, "then perhaps it's time to call things off."

"Break up?!" Shuichi yelled, grabbing Suguru by the shoulders and shaking him violently. "How can you even say that?!"

"Oh, no, that's not what I meant." Suguru scrambled to explain himself, but Shuichi had moved his hands up to strangle him.

"In other words," Hiro said, "all of us in Bad Luck hope you manage to find a way to make your love grow." He flipped his hair and winked at the hostess even though this was radio and nobody could see him.

Suguru's noble sacrifice had torn Shuichi's attention away from ranting about his lover. If they fled now, there was a good chance they could survive the program in one piece.

The hostess' professional instincts kicked in. "Right, thank you, everyone. Today's guests were the members of Bad Luck. Tonight's final musical selection is a number that perfectly matches an evening like this one. Requested by "Oh Dear" as well as many others, a bittersweet love song from Bad Luck's first album."

The song started with a melodious intro followed by Shuichi's voice. The hostess couldn't believe the same three people who had nearly trashed the studio a few minutes before had been able to record such a beautiful song.

But they had done it by pouring their souls into their work. On the recording, Hiro played his guitar expertly. Suguru's arrangements really brought the song together, and Shuichi's voice mesmerized the listeners with its strength and beauty.

Despite their youth and the trouble they often found themselves in, Hiro, Suguru, and Shuichi were truly talented musicians. Bad Luck was making a big splash in the music industry.

"I'm home!" Shuichi yelled when he got to Yuki's apartment after the radio show, but there was a slight tremble to his otherwise powerful voice.

He had already forgotten all the problems he'd caused for his band and his producer at the radio station. The only thing he could think of was Yuki, who he expected would be finished with his work and eagerly waiting for him.

From the street, Shuichi had seen that all the lights were off. When he stepped in, it was totally silent. He assumed Yuki was sound asleep after pulling an all-nighter, and he was glad he had resisted the urge to call.

Careful to be quiet, he snuck down the hall toward the bedroom. Peering at the bed, he whispered, "Yuki, I missed you so much."

He congratulated himself on being so mature. When they had first begun dating, Shuichi wouldn't have been able to control his excitement.

He would have burst through the door, knocking it off its hinges. He would have shouted loud enough to shake the walls, before jumping on top of Yuki. Maybe he had learned from all the times Yuki had punched, kicked, or thrown him into the wall in retaliation.

"I thought of nothing but you," Shuichi announced.

The smells that Shuichi associated with his lover—the lingering scent of his shampoo, the permanent odor of his cigarettes, even the smell of the half-read book by the bedside table—all of these aromas filled Shuichi's heart with joy. For days these fragrances had been missing from his life, so he breathed them in deeply, filling his lungs to capacity, until he was almost drunk from happiness.

"Oh, Yuki," he sighed, settling into bed. He wriggled through the covers toward his beloved. His outstretched hand touched something hard.

"Wah!" He jerked back too far, hitting his head against the wall. Then he rolled reflexively in the opposite direction and fell onto the floor.

"Yuki?"

He leapt up and yanked the covers off the bed. There was no one there. In the dark, he'd assumed Yuki was asleep, but perhaps he was hiding somewhere, playing a practical joke.

"Trying to surprise me? I never thought you'd be this naughty!" Shuichi giggled, beginning to search the other rooms. He peeked inside every closet and cabinet, even inside the suitcases, but Yuki wasn't there.

He was baffled. When he'd called home after the radio show, Yuki hadn't answered the land line or his cell. Shuichi had assumed Yuki was working or sleeping, but maybe he'd been out driving.

"Maybe he wanted to make a special dinner for me and had to go shopping!"

The thought of Yuki's cooking made all his tension melt away. His lover was amazing at everything he did—especially cooking. Every time he ate one of Yuki's meals, he tasted a secret ingredient: love.

"A candlelight dinner! At last, Yuki is being romantic! I wonder what he's going to cook?"

But when he dialed Yuki's mobile phone, it went right to voice mail.

"Um, it's me," he said. "I just got home, but you're not here. Please call! I'll wait up . . ." His voice gradually petered out.

Something's wrong. This isn't the way things were supposed to turn out. Shuichi's good mood drifted into serious concern. He'd told Yuki over and over again that he'd be home today.

Yuki had said, "Okay, fine. I'll be in bed." Shuichi had been so overjoyed he had flung his arms around the older man and hugged Yuki as tightly as he could. Of course, Yuki had added, "By which I mean I'll be sleeping."

Shuichi had been looking forward to gazing at his lover's sleeping face, but now there was nothing but an empty bed. He was forced to sit and wait for Yuki to call.

"Where the hell did you go?"

Each tick of the clock sounded like a hammer pounding. He glared at it, convinced that an incredibly long time had passed, but it had been only ten minutes. Unable to wait any longer, he hit redial. He got Yuki's voice mail again.

"You were up all night. How can you be out?" he demanded.

Yuki'd had a deadline yesterday, which always meant at least one night without sleep. Maybe more. For him to leave home in that condition was proof that lack of sleep had impaired his judgment.

Shuichi was plagued by terrible thoughts. *What if Yuki fell asleep when driving and had a horrible car accident?! What if Yuki fell asleep on the side of a road and was kidnapped by a raving lunatic?! What if Yuki fell asleep while driving on a bridge, drove into the sea, and was eaten by bloodthirsty sharks?!*

"Argh!" he yelled, tearing at his hair. "Please, Yuki! I don't have to touch you! Just to see your face—just to hear your voice! That's enough for me! I'm begging you! Let me know you're alive!"

But the room was silent; the echoes of his voice faded away, his prayers unanswered.

TICK, TOCK. TICK, TOCK.

Not only was the clock unbearable, but Shuichi was listening for the sound of the phone so intently that the refrigerator's hum was deafening. And he was sure he could even hear the sound of the hour hand as it swept across the dial.

"Yuki, where are you?" he whispered.

Shuichi was almost never in their apartment by himself. Even when Yuki was working, Shuichi could hear his lover's fingers tapping on the keyboard or his grumbling while he crumpled up notepaper. Those sounds were reassuring, but this silence was nerveracking.

"Yuki, you promised!" His heart sank. He shook his head violently, driving away the temptation to blame his absent lover. "At least call! I'm worried!"

He pulled out his cell phone and stared at it, willing it to ring. Yuki had not responded to any of the hundreds of e-mails Shuichi had fired off from all over the country. *Maybe he fell off a cliff days ago and no one knows to look for his body?*

Just as he was really starting to panic, his phone made a tiny little noise. He pressed the answer button even before his ring tone started and shouted into the phone.

"Where the hell are you? I was very worried!"

"Oh, I'm sorry," came a very calm voice.

"President?" Shuichi deflated. It was Tohma, the president of N-G Pro. Shuichi reflexively bowed his head to apologize. "Sorry, I thought you were . . ."

"Yuki?"

"Yeah," Shuichi said.

"I heard the radio show. Keep that high level of energy going tomorrow," Tohma said cheerfully.

"Do you know where Yuki is?"

Tohma paused. "Have you looked around carefully?"

"He's nowhere!" Shuichi said, irritated.

Tohma didn't reply.

"Hello?" Shuichi said, his instincts telling him to be cautious since Tohma was in the middle of thinking about something. "Can you help me, Tohma?"

"Well," he said with false reluctance. "When I saw him, he was with a woman. She was *very* dressed up."

Shuichi froze, unable to breathe. *Tohma spotted Yuki cheating on me?*

"What?!" He exploded. "Who? I won't let some . . . some *woman* come between me and Yuki! Who was she? You have to tell me!"

"Hm . . . Good question."

Shuichi ground his teeth. Tohma always did this. "Where'd you see Yuki and this . . . this woman?"

"Now, I couldn't possibly tell you *that,*" Tohma said slyly.

Shuichi felt like all the air had been knocked out of him. *It couldn't be . . . There was no way he'd gone to a hotel . . . and made love? With some dressed up hussy?*

Fingers tightening around the phone, Shuichi tried his best to calm his thundering pulse.

He was only further disheartened by Tohma's cheery voice. "I'm looking forward to Osaka tomorrow, Shindou. See you there!"

Realizing the man was about to hang up, Shuichi hurriedly said, "Wait a second!"

A brief pause, then, "Yes?"

Tohma always got perturbed when anything connected to Yuki came up, so his casual tone seemed very suspicious.

"Are you . . . possibly . . . against our relationship?"

Shuichi understood that he put Tohma in a rough spot. A male musician from his agency dating another man, and not just any man but a bestselling author, was probably not the ideal situation from a business standpoint, especially since neither Shuichi nor Yuki had made much effort to hide their relationship. And then there was also the fact that Yuki was Tohma's brother-in-law.

"Not at all," Tohma said lightly, but Shuichi was still suspicious. Everyone at N-G Pro knew how unpredictable Tohma was when he acted cheerful. "I respect Yuki's freedom. He's family, after all."

"So, um . . ." Shuichi searched for the right words.

"Don't worry. He always handled his affairs with the utmost discretion . . . until he met you."

"I'm not worried about bad publicity." Shuichi suddenly felt like a wife with a malicious mother-in-law.

"Get some rest tonight, okay?" Tohma encouraged. "We want to make a big splash in Osaka."

"Of course! I'm really looking forward to it!" Shuichi said, bowing his head. He made sure to wait for Tohma to hang up before he did.

"What's going on?" Shuichi wondered. "Yuki's freedom . . . freedom with that very dressed up *woman?*"

He didn't want to think about that. He wished he could believe in Yuki, but, unfortunately, he couldn't help but be suspicious of his gorgeous lover. Yuki was sometimes too receptive to the attention that women gave him—and there were so many women always giving him attention! *Yuki could have almost any woman in Japan.*

"Yuki!" Shuichi paced the room like a caged tiger. "Here I thought you'd fallen asleep while driving or fallen off a cliff. I was worried sick!

But no, you're with this . . . this . . . dressed up woman!"

Suddenly, a thought struck him. *Were you so lonely without me that you had to have an affair? You wouldn't do that, would you?*

"Please, somebody tell me I'm wrong!" Shuichi began racing frantically around the apartment. He banged his little toe on the edge of his lover's desk. He rolled on the floor, holding his foot, after letting loose a shout so loud it could have brought an audience of thousands to their feet.

As he lay on the floor, a single piece of paper, dislodged when he kicked the desk, fluttered down to land on his face. Ignoring the throbbing pain, he grabbed the paper which was emblazoned with the logo "Kunoichi," and as he did, he caught a whiff of sweet-smelling perfume.

"Huh?"

Shuichi thought the scent was familiar, but before he could remember where he'd smelled it, he saw what was written on the note.

It was like a dagger straight to his heart.

"What?!" he shrieked, leaping upright and glaring at the note. He read it over and over again, but the words didn't change. He read it out loud.

"I've taken Yuki. Just in case."

From the handwriting, Shuichi knew that a woman had written the note. He immediately assumed the worst. *This woman and Yuki!*

His fist clenched unconsciously, crumpling up the paper.

"Just in case! What the heck does that mean? Just in case *of what?*" Shuichi cried, latching onto that trivial detail because he didn't want to think about what was happening.

"Just in case," Shuichi repeated. *I was right! Yuki has been kidnapped by a raving lunatic.*

"Oh, Yuki! It would be better if you were lying somewhere helpless and no one could find you!"

Shuichi was confused because Yuki was always so guarded and careful. *How did this woman lure him away?* It must have been harder than taming a wild animal. Even the famous zookeeper Mitsugorou would've had trouble talking him into anything.

"That woman Tohma mentioned—could she have seduced him?"

I was gone too long, and he got lonely. I'm sorry, Yuki! It's all my fault! If I had stayed near you instead of going on tour, this would've never happened!

"Just in case," Shuichi said over and over. "What the hell does that mean?!" he screamed. Suddenly, his mobile phone rang. He glanced at the screen; it was a number he didn't recognize.

It must be the kidnapper! He gulped. *The lights are on in the room, so she knows I'm home!* His stomach dropped. Shuichi took three long breaths and forced his heart to slow before he finally answered the phone.

"Okay! Okay!" he cried into the phone, moaning. "What are your demands?"

He could pay the ransom. And if he didn't have enough money, he could try to pay in installments, to work it off for the rest of his life. Even if the kidnapper wanted him to perform naked, that was fine. Anything, as long as she gave Yuki back.

But what if it's Yuki she wants? Rivers of sweat poured down his face. *First I have to find out if*

Yuki is okay. And where he's being kept! Suddenly, a voice cut through Shuichi's resolve. It sounded unexpectedly amused.

"Demands? Well, that does save me some time."

"Time?" *What? Wait a second!* Shuichi knew that voice. It was nearly identical to Yuki's. "Tatsuha?"

"Yep, it's me." Tatsuha was Yuki's brother. "Your favorite Buddhist monk from Kyoto!"

"I know. But I don't have time for you now! Your . . . Yuki . . . terrible . . ."

Shuichi was tongue-tied. But he was always fumbling over words, so Tatsuha didn't notice.

"How's it going? I guess you know why I'm calling, given the timing. Huh, Shu-Shu?"

"What?" Shuichi asked, confused. *Tatsuha's involved in the kidnapping?* "You're working for the woman who stole Yuki?"

"Stole? You're crazy. He's holed up in some hotel room in Osaka."

"What? She's locked him up in a hotel room? In Osaka?" Shuichi's brain was turning to mush.

"Look, Shu-Shu, I don't know what's up with you, but your loverboy's over here doing research or something. Too bad for you, huh? Even though your concert's so close." Tatsuha seemed to think Shuichi was in Osaka as well. "Both of you are working so hard. Of course, at least my brother's got a gorgeous lady editor to keep him company."

"Gorgeous lady . . ." Shuichi blinked rapidly.

Tohma had said Yuki was with a woman who was dressed up, and now Tatsuha said she was gorgeous.

"He's not one to say no to a lady," Tatsuha said. "Too bad for you, though." He started chanting a sutra.

"Shut up!" Shuichi yelled.

"Hey, you should count yourself lucky. People *pay* me to chant for them! I hit ten stages a day during the *obon* season, you know."

"Nobody asked about your schedule!" Shuichi snarled. "Where's Yuki?"

"You're his lover. If you don't know, how the hell should I?"

"Oh!" Shuichi felt a sharp ache in his chest, but Tatsuha pressed on, happy as ever.

"Well, I feel for you, Shu-Shu. To cheer you up, I'm gonna swing by your dressing room!"

Shuichi no longer had the energy to refuse.

"Uh-huh, sure. Whatever. Nittle Grasper's dressing room has very tight security," Shuichi reminded him. "But I'll make sure you get to talk to Ryuichi in Osaka."

Tatsuha was obsessed with Ryuichi Sakuma, the lead singer of Nittle Grasper, Japan's most popular band. Ryuichi was considered one of the best singers in the world and was Shuichi's role model.

The priest cackled. "I'll hold you to that."

If I'm not too busy looking for Yuki, that is. But before he could say that, Tatsuha hung up. *Both brothers are so selfish!*

If Yuki was planning on going to Osaka for work, why didn't he just say so? I wouldn't have had to push so hard to come back to Tokyo. Everything would've been easier. We could've just hooked up in Osaka and had more time together.

His shoulders slumped, but he was also extremely relieved that Yuki hadn't been kidnapped. *Maybe he went to Osaka just to visit me?*

"But he'd never admit it. For a romance novelist, he gets so embarrassed with stuff like that." Shuichi purred as he slid into the realm of fantasy.

He made what he imagined to be a rather nihilistic, Yuki-like expression. "This is for work," he said curtly, mimicking Yuki. *Hah! Pretending that his trip to Osaka wasn't just to see me.* It didn't sound anything like Yuki, but because of his desperate longing, Shuichi believed it. He shrieked like a schoolgirl, blushed, and thumped his fist on the wall excitedly.

"Perfect! Perfect!" He congratulated himself, chuckling as he skipped out of the office.

If Shuichi's lover had been there to see his goofy smile, he would undoubtedly have kicked him as hard as he could. Shuichi's birdbrain was filled with love, love for a cold man who was always less than affectionate, expressing his feelings only as an afterthought. To Shuichi, those infrequent, miraculous gestures of love made it all worthwhile.

"Yuki!" Shuichi shouted before resting in bed and falling quickly asleep. Surrounded by the evocative scent of his lover, he spun passion-filled dreams that night. And perhaps Yuki would be waiting for him to arrive in Osaka tomorrow. Perhaps Yuki would take him on a wonderful, romantic date. Maybe Yuki would swing by the dressing room before the show, give him a good luck kiss, and after the concert he'd tell Shuichi what a good job he'd done on-stage.

Of course these were nothing but dreams brought about by his lover's fragrance and his overactive imagination. The toe he'd banged on the desk was turning red, but the endorphins that his brain secreted masked the pain and allowed him to dream in peace.

When he woke the next morning, he felt completely refreshed, having gotten the best sleep he'd had in months.

"Here I come, Osaka! Here I come, Yuki!"

GRAVITATION: Voice of Temptation

Shuichi's desperate worries from the night
before were gone. He leapt out of bed and ran out
the door, excited to start the day.

Unfortunately, he failed to notice the other
note that had been left for him. It lay on the floor
of the apartment after he was gone, a footprint
stamped over the words.

Track Two:
The Unanswered Phone

Shuichi and Bad Luck had taken the bullet train back to Osaka and were hanging around the Ebisu Bridge, also known as the Pickup Bridge. Despite the bustle of the crowd around them, Hiro was able to hear his ring tone. When he saw who was calling, he tried, unsuccessfully, to appear casual when he answered.

"Uh, hey! It's been a long time. I, uh . . . Wow! I'm so happy to hear your voice!" Hiro was bubbling with excitement. It was obvious that it was his girlfriend, calling from Kyoto. "Yeah, I'm in Osaka. I really, *really* want to see you. I wanna skip rehearsals and come over there right now!"

(Shuichi was by no means the only one who could ooze love.)

"What?" Hiro asked. "No, of course I can't actually *do* that, but that's how I feel! Right, ha ha ha!" Sensing Shuichi's reproachful gaze, Hiro abandoned the very notion of skipping rehearsals.

"Oh? Really? No, absolutely! Anytime! That means we'll be able to spend more time together. I'm looking forward to it. I'll e-mail you directions—oh, you already know where it is? But the dressing room's . . . What? Where am I now? Osaka! Didn't I say?" Hiro suddenly stiffened, becoming hesitant. "Where in Osaka? Um, I don't really know. Some place that's on TV a lot."

"Pickup Bridge!" Shuichi shouted, clinging to Hiro's back. "Know why they call it that? Because guys come here to pick up girls! It's the most famous pick up spot in Osaka! Hah!"

"No! Of course I'm not trying to pick up girls! We're just meeting . . . Uh, hello? Ayaka? Hello!" She had hung up. Hiro made a fist around his disconnected phone and swung it at his partner. "Shuichi! Stop trying to get me in trouble!"

"What? I was just saying where we were!"

"Yeah, but she didn't need to know why guys come here!"

Shuichi didn't answer; instead he just smiled at Hiro.

The stone bridge over Dotonbori River usually thronged with tourists and shoppers, but luckily it was still early and there weren't a lot of people around. The dozens who were there milled around, staring at Bad Luck.

Shuichi was suction-cupped to Hiro, the one person who would pay any attention to him. K was getting his picture taken in front of the Glico sign and, for some reason, was standing in the *inochi* pose, making the symbol for "life" with his arms and legs. Their producer, Sakano, was sighing as if a piece of his soul were being torn away as he took each picture. There was no sign of Suguru anywhere, which just meant he was, as usual, doing a very good job of pretending he wasn't with the rest of them.

"You have the nerve to take a romantic call when *my* lover's missing?" Shuichi sniffled.

Shuichi had assumed that when he arrived in Osaka, he'd be able to see Yuki—despite having no way to get in touch with the man. That had been the one thing keeping his spirits up. But no matter how many times he called, Yuki didn't answer his cell. Instead, a woman's voice came on the line and said calmly, "This phone is turned off or out of range. Please try again later." Shuichi tried e-mailing him, but Yuki had yet to respond.

"Why?" Shuichi shrieked.

Hiro didn't know what to say. He quickly tried to think of a way to help. "You know he's in a hotel in Osaka, right?" Hiro asked.

"Hotel, motel, capsule hotel, inn, resort, bed and breakfast, lodge, crack house. He could be anywhere!" Shuichi sighed gloomily as he looked through the listings for hotels he had torn out of the yellow pages from inside a phone booth. "How do I find you, Yuki? Where can you be? And what the hell are you up to?!" Letting his anger get the better of him, he tore the listings to shreds and threw them in the air. They floated down like confetti while Hiro scrambled around, picking them up.

"Kids, don't try this at home!" Hiro cried, but his reproach had little effect.

"The whole reason for having this cell is to talk to you anytime!" Shuichi stared at his phone. "Call me! Or at least send me a text message!"

Yuki had insisted he didn't need his own mobile phone since he always worked at home. But Shuichi had demanded that he buy one.

"Why aren't you calling me back?" Shuichi growled, flinging the phone down at the stone bridge. It was the first time he'd let go of it all morning.

"If you break it, he'll never get through," Hiro pointed out.

Shuichi hurriedly picked it up and rubbed it against his cheek. "I'm so sorry! Please forgive me!" He brushed an invisible speck of dust off it, polished it with his handkerchief and kissed it. "I'm begging you, connect me to Yuki! Please!"

"No matter how much you beg," Hiro said, "unless Yuki turns his phone on . . ."

"Hiro!" Shuichi cried, flinging his arms around his friend. "Am I so ugly?" A cascade of tears burst from his eyes and ran down Hiro's shirt.

Despite the fact that Shuichi had just messed things up with Hiro's girlfriend, he did his best to help. "Um, well . . . male beauty's not really my area of expertise, but . . ."

"I haven't seen him for days! Now I can't even talk to him! I'm about to lose my mind!"

"About to?" Hiro said.

Shuichi wailed, "Of course! It's *normal* to be a mess!"

"Um, yeah . . ."

The singer pouted. "So cold. You don't love me?"

By this point a crowd was beginning to close in around them. Since they had no way of knowing that Shuichi was speaking to someone who wasn't there, they must have assumed it was a lovers' quarrel. A crowd of paparazzi started taking pictures, and a lot of the tourists joined in.

"Well," Hiro sighed. He turned to face Shuichi. "You said he was stuck in a hotel room, right? So, like, he's being quarantined?"

"Don't talk about him like he's got some horrible virus!" Shuichi shouted, head-butting Hiro in the chin and knocking him down.

Although he lay collapsed on the ground, Hiro continued to lecture Shuichi. "Have you considered Yuki's feelings? I mean, maybe he wants to see you, but he just can't get away."

"Really?" Shuichi gaped at Hiro. He was so used to being the emotional one that it hadn't occurred to him that Yuki might be also feeling lonely right at this moment. *Hiro's right. It must be true! Because we're in love!*

Still on the ground, Hiro watched as Shuichi swooned.

"He's probably trying his best to call you but just can't."

"That explains everything!" Shuichi knelt down on one knee. Tears gushed from his eyes as he took his friend's hand. "It was all my fault! I said I'd love him no matter what, yet my heart was weak."

The crowd burst into applause.

"Beautiful, man!"

"Stay strong!"

"We've got your back!"

"Go for it!"

The audience, the applause, and the cheers lifted Shuichi's spirits and triggered something in his mind.

"Thank you, thank you," he said, springing to his feet and waving at the crowd. "Thank you, everyone! You give me strength. Without my fans, I'm nothing!"

His power restored, Shuichi vowed not to worry too much about Yuki.

The crowd shouted with glee, carried away with emotion. They felt so overjoyed that they grabbed Shuichi and tossed him in the air. His tiny body flew up into the blue Osaka sky.

"What the hell is going on?" Suguru demanded, returning with his hands full of steaming octopus dumplings called *takoyaki*.

Shuichi landed at his feet, immensely satisfied. "Oh, Suguru! I love to play live! The audience's feelings are like a wave that I can ride—it's like surfing on the sea!"

"But we haven't performed yet," Suguru said, still confused.

"I don't care, as long as they're happy! Manager! Let's take over the Osaka Castle!"

"I do hate to correct you," Sakano interrupted. "But it's the Osaka Castle *Hall.*"

Shuichi wasn't listening. "Osaka Castle! How can we go wrong in a venue with a name like that? We're gonna conquer the world!" He laughed as he got another round of applause from the adoring crowd. The attention fired him up even more. He darted over to his manager.

"Let's move! Let's go! Where are we going next?"

"Shuichi!" K said. "I've got something to show you!"

Sakano, Suguru, and Hiro all stiffened, nervous by the excessive glee in K's blue eyes.

"Ho ho ho! I thought something like this might happen, so I planted a special transceiver! I can pinpoint the exact location anytime I want!"

"Transceiver?" Shuichi's head snapped around, his priorities quickly reordered. "On Yuki? You know where Yuki is?"

K opened a laptop in front of Shuichi's bulging eyes. A satellite photo of the city appeared on a screen framed within a window surrounded by military jargon.

Shuichi pointed happily at a small flashing light. "Is this him? Where is that? Where is he?"

"Let's see . . . on top of Ebisu Bridge!"

"What? Where?" Shuichi looked around. There was no sign of Yuki. "I don't see him," he howled. "Where is he?"

K pointed at him. "In between your teeth!"

"What? You mean the tracking chip? You got my hopes up for nothing! And you messed with my body!"

"Shuichi!" Sakano cried, turning white, his fierce loyalty to N-G Pro the only thing keeping him from passing out. "We should get going. Why don't we head to Osaka Castle, like you said?" The Osaka Castle Hall was right next to Osaka Castle, so Sakano just gave up correcting Shuichi.

"I just summoned transport," K said. "It should arrive momentarily." He planted his long legs on the railing, standing like a sailor. "I set it on the fastest route possible."

"You mean with a car navigation system?" Hiro asked.

"That uses a military satellite?" Suguru added, worried.

Both of them felt nervous. They imagined a tank or other armored riot vehicle crushing the cars that were double-parked all along the adjacent boulevards.

"Attention, everyone!" K fired his gun several times into the air. "Time to move to our next location!"

Bad Luck was in the middle of a ridiculous schedule—a combination of tourism, meetings, and press junkets. They were going to swing by America Mura and Universal Studios Japan later in the day.

Hiro and the others had agreed to the plan, thinking it would cheer Shuichi up, but now everyone was beginning to have second thoughts. It almost seemed as though all of this was designed simply for K's entertainment.

"Well, while we wait, let's eat these takoyaki," Suguru suggested, passing the dumplings around.

"I'll eat anything!" Shuichi cried, grapping a toothpick quickly tossing a bunch of dumplings into his mouth. "Ha-ha-hot!" He ran around clutching his throat.

Sakano whipped out a thermos of tea. "Shuichi! Quick! Drink this!"

Shuichi grabbed it, dumped the entire contents down his throat, and then ran around twice as fast. "Waaaaaah! I'm on fire!"

"No need to rush through it, Shuichi. It's not a race," Sakano said.

"That's what you get for scarfing it all!" Suguru snatched the tray of dumplings back from Shuichi as he ran past. "If you burn your tongue or throat, you won't be able to perform tonight!"

"So we'd better eat the rest of these for you," Hiro added quickly, taking the tray like a baton in a relay race and piercing a dumpling with a toothpick.

Shuichi ran to Hiro and yanked at his long hair.

"At least let me have one, Shuichi."

"The tea . . . It's hot . . . But it's not that it's hot . . ."

"What?" Suguru asked, munching on the dumplings.

"It's hot, but more importantly, it's really, really *gross.*"

"Bitter tea is better for you," Sakano said. "Being on tour wears you out, but it would never do for you to weaken or get sick." There was a purely coincidental flash of light of Sakano's glasses that made him look sinister. "It's special medicinal tea. I trust you liked it?"

"I just said it was gross! Medicinal tea, my foot! That's six levels beyond chameleon plant or turmeric! What the hell is it?"

"I cannot tell you. It's a secret."

Shuichi yelled, enraged, and flung the thermos at Sakano, hitting the man in the head.

"Watch your mouth! Be careful what you say in the meeting!" K cautioned, stuffing a half-dozen dumplings in his face so rapidly that his cheeks bulged like a hamster's.

"Americans sure do eat a lot," Hiro noted, staring dismally at the empty tray in his hand. K had wolfed everything down.

When he saw that, Shuichi screamed, "Give me back my dumplings!" He snatched one from Suguru. "My dumplings! I only got to eat a few!"

"You do remember that *I* bought them, right?" Suguru asked.

"We're all in the same band. Your things, my things, it's all the same."

"Well, at least you *think* like a team," Sakano said, forlornly sipping a different tea than the one he'd given to Shuichi.

Bad Luck continued arguing over the waters of the Dotonbori River. Gradually, all the shops on the street opened, and more and more people flocked to the area.

Suguru heard a small noise beneath the flurry of Kansai dialect around them.

"Someone's phone is ringing," he said. "But I don't know that melody."

Shuichi glanced at his phone. "Oh!"

He had set his phone to ring with *that* tone only when one special person called. "Yuki! You do love me!" He shook as he tried to answer, but K kicked the phone right out of his trembling hand.

"Turn that thing off! We're working!" the American bellowed.

"Aaah!" Shuichi shrieked, diving after the phone as it flew through the air over the edge of the bridge.

"Yuki! Wait! Don't hang up!"

"Shuichi, stop!" Hiro cried, but he was too late.

Shuichi dove into the river after the cell phone, making an enormous splash.

"Eeek! Shuichi jumped!" Someone shrieked from the bridge.

"We'll follow him!" Several of the girls that had been watching from a distance leapt into the river after him. "Hang on, Shuichi!"

"I'll save you, Shuichi!"

"Let me touch you, Shuichi!"

One after another, they flocked to Shuichi, as if trying to drown him. In the confusion, their hands roamed all over his body. Unable to call for help without swallowing water, he shook off one of the girls clinging to him . . . but was instantly grabbed by another. As Shuichi reenacted the demise of the Titanic, a rope borrowed from the nearby rescue box fell toward him.

"Grab this, Shuichi!" Suguru cried, causing even more commotion.

A group of old men leaned over the railing.

"What? Huh?" one of them groaned.

"Must be some sort of TV program," another muttered.

"Young people these days . . ."

One body after another spilled over the edge, with the same sort of mass hysteria one would expect to see when the Tigers won the series or when Japan advanced to the finals of the world cup. Though this was likely the first recorded case in which girls were among the jumpers.

"Hey, people, don't jump into the river! It's polluted and full of E. coli! Please, stop!" a policeman shouted, but, like an avalanche, people kept spilling over the railing into the river. They didn't have any idea what was waiting for them below, but they were caught up in the moment. A few even managed graceful, Olympic-quality dives.

"Those Osakans! They'll risk their lives for a gag. Gotta respect that," Hiro muttered, watching as people dove on his drowning partner.

"But at this rate, Shuichi may never surface again!" Sakano wailed.

"Don't worry! Shuichi's tougher than he looks. Otherwise, I'd never work with him," K said calmly, dangling a fishing line over the railing. Despite his constant insistence that his job was to protect his musicians, he was just hanging out, doing nothing but watching the melee.

"Don't just stand there, K! Do something! Save Shuichi!" Sakano cried, so agitated he wound up doing a nervous dance on the railing.

Just then, the surface of the water began to bubble. With a sinister rumble, a massive shadow rose from the depths. The screaming crowd fell silent. The fangirls and old men quickly swam for shore.

The only one left in the water was Shuichi, flailing his arms and gasping for breath.

"Shuichi!" Hiro yelled. "Get out of there!"

"Help!" Shuichi yelled as he saw the huge, black darkness gliding under him, rising up. First, a projection like a dorsal fin appeared. It was followed by the clear outline of a glistening body and tail, streamlined and black.

Shuichi blinked. *A shark?* He couldn't believe his eyes. How could he possibly be seeing this shape in Japan, in Osaka, in such a shallow, narrow river?

"J-Jaws?" *It's gonna eat me! I'm dead! Oh, my beautiful Yuki!* The face of his beloved flashed before his eyes.

But Shuichi loved more than just Yuki's face. He loved Yuki's soft, pale skin. He loved those arms and that chest. He even loved Yuki's sharp words and cold heart. He loved Yuki's beauty and all of his faults. Shuichi's memories flashed in his mind's eye, twirling and morphing like the view from a kaleidoscope.

"Yuki," he cried. "I'm sorry. I'm *so* sorry." *You finally called, and I'm gonna die without getting a chance to answer! I was your lover, but now I'm just fish food! And I'll never see you again.*

Pushing a great wave before it, the black thing came closer.

"Make it fast," Shuichi said. "Eat me quick." He closed his eyes tightly, awaiting his end. But the shark didn't attack. It picked him up on the tip of its nose.

"I *said,* hurry up and eat me!" he cried, flinging his arms and legs out, but the sensation pressing against his back was not quite what he'd expected. *It's hard. It's very hard. Like iron.*

His eyes snapped open, and he stared down at the behemoth. "A submarine?"

What the heck is this submarine doing in Dotonbori River?

"What is this? A movie? You need permission to film here, you know," the policeman said to Sakano. "Are you in charge?"

"Oh, yes, I am! I am so terribly sorry! Please don't give me a ticket! I'll get it out of here immediately!"

"Let's go!" K shouted.

He shoved Hiro, Suguru, and Sakano over the rail. They screamed on the fall down, then landed safely on top of the submarine. Bad Luck swiftly boarded. The vessel descended below the surface of the river and was gone.

"Oh no!" Shuichi shivered violently inside the submarine, but not because he was soaking wet, not because he had nearly drowned, and not because he had been hauled onboard a mysterious submarine. He was shivering because the mobile phone he had risked his life to rescue was broken.

"Yuki called me back at last, and it's like I hung up on him without saying anything! Even if he does call me again, he'll think I've turned it off! He'll think I don't want to talk to him!"

Shuichi stuck one arm out of the blanket he was wrapped in, striking a pose like the undercover samurai on *Toyama no Kin-san.* "Hiro! Bringeth thy cell phone!"

Shuichi quickly dialed Yuki's number. He often forgot his parents' number, but he could never forget Yuki's. Unfortunately, Yuki's phone went straight to voice mail.

"What the hell is going *on?* You just called!" Shuichi shouted, punching redial over and over again.

He kept trying in vain on the way to Universal Studios—where K went wild, dragging them all over the theme park while Shuichi kept trying to reach Yuki. His beloved never answered.

Finally, when they were back in the submarine, the battery ran out, and Shuichi gave the cell back to Hiro.

"Don't worry, Shuichi," Hiro said, trying to make him feel better.

"You'll get in touch with him eventually," Suguru added.

"No. He won't call again," Shuichi said, and then all of a sudden, he grinned.

His companions backed off hurriedly. They'd been with him so long that they could sense when his thoughts crossed over into dangerous territory.

"I think I know what happened!" Shuichi shouted. "He was only able to phone when this dressed up lady editor who has him locked away went to the bathroom. But she came back out and caught him making the call. Then she took away his phone and increased the security around him!"

"Um, that sounds pretty unlikely," Suguru said.

"Like something out of a thriller," Hiro added.

Shuichi was in a world of his own and didn't hear them.

"Yuki risked it all trying to call me. But just when he got through . . ." Shuichi wiped away his tears. They were tears of joy. He hadn't been able to answer, but what was important was that Yuki had tried.

"I can feel the warmth of your heart!" Shuichi yelled. "It's lit a fire in me that all the water in the Dotonbori can't put out!" He thumped his fist on his chest, then started thinking out loud. "Yuki has his excessively well-dressed female editor, I have a well-armed American manager, and both of them are getting in our way!"

Shuichi's eyebrows creased. He gazed up into the tiny lamp fixed in the roof of the submarine like he was on stage and it was a spotlight. He reached one hand toward the light, did a little tap dance, and crossed both hands over his chest.

"That editor and K are keeping us apart like we're a modern-day Romeo and Juliet!" Shuichi raved. "I'll sing loud enough to reach your ears, Yuki. I'll fill all of Osaka with my love!" He spun back toward his comrades and screamed, *"Yukiiiiiii!"*

Suddenly, Shuichi was thrust into darkness. It was as if the lamp had become disgusted with his melodramatic acting and decided to switch off and ignore him.

Shuichi had been shouting at the top of his lungs in the very cramped space, so everyone's ears were ringing. They all thought Shuichi was pretending, that he was being overly dramatic as usual, but he was utterly serious.

Eventually, the mysterious submarine sur-faced. The members of Bad Luck got out and walked into Osaka Castle Hall.

♩ ♪ ♩ ♩ ♪ ♩ ♩ ♪ ♩ ♩

That evening, after the dress rehearsal, Bad Luck's waiting room hummed with tension. Shuichi usually became more excited as a performance neared, running around like a chicken with its head cut off, but today he was sitting in miserable silence. His grief shrouded the room in darkness.

"Yuki," Shuichi whispered desperately.

Hiro's long hair was bound back; there wasn't a trace of his trademark smile on his face. He tuned his guitar, obsessively checking each string, never once looking up.

Suguru's nimble fingers swept over his keyboard. He was so small that he could be mistaken for an elementary school student, but he was playing Liszt with the skill of a veteran classical pianist. Franz Liszt apparently had extremely long fingers and was famous for making pianists weep with his frequent demands for them to reach across distances far greater than was reasonable. On a piano, one could use the pedal to extend the sound and cover for this, but to play Liszt successfully on a keyboard was much more difficult. By doing so, Suguru was displaying his true genius.

Unfortunately, the source of their incredible concentration came less from their devotion to music than their fervent desire to avoid eye contact with the bleak banshee sitting next to them.

"Oh, Yuki," Shuichi sighed. *Even if we can't be together, our hearts are one.* "Doing my job well means fighting by your side." A blinding light shone from Shuichi's eyes. His pupils smoldered like twin volcanoes.

Too much had happened the last couple of days. His brain had been in overdrive and was burning out. It was now twisting the facts to suit its own purposes.

"Oh, I burn for you, Yuki!" Shuichi shouted.

Someone suddenly stuck a lighter in his face and set his bangs on fire. There was only one man who would pull a stunt like that.

"You trying to burn me bald before the show?" Shuichi screamed. "What did I ever do to you?"

"Relax," his manager said unapologetically. "Just going with the flow."

So when K sees someone metaphorically burning, he feels like literally setting them on fire? Or is it just an immensely stupid joke? Either way, K had clearly been the only one getting a kick out of Shuichi's strange mood.

Just then, Sakano returned to the waiting room. He had received a phone call a little earlier and had left to meet someone.

"This gentlemen requested that I escort him here," Sakano announced, indicating someone just beyond the door.

"Yuki?" Shuichi flung his producer aside, looking for his lover.

In his fervor, Shuichi accidentally slammed Sakano face-first into the wall. The producer crumbled in a heap on the floor, his glasses broken, but Shuichi didn't notice because he was too busy tackling the tall man standing in the hallway.

Track Two: The Unanswered Phone

"You came to meet me since I wasn't answering my phone? You risked your life escaping from your captor? Oh! I'm gonna die from happiness!" Shuichi wailed, clinging to the man's chest.

But then a smooth voice soothed him, "You can die, but only after you keep your promise."

Shuichi's head snapped up.

"Judging from your warm welcome, you must have good news for me," Tatsuha said, grinning down at him.

"You're not Yuki!" he spat out, letting go and backing away in disgust.

Tatsuha looked like he could be Yuki's identical twin, but his features were darker. He flipped back his hair (which was much too long for a priest) exactly the same way Yuki did, but somehow Yuki's movements were always more elegant. Tatsuha's eyes flashed with mischief, but not as sharply as Yuki's. They didn't gleam and pierce Shuichi's heart. Yuki's skin was white like cream and silky smooth. Their voices were similar, but no one had lips like Yuki's. Shuichi wanted nothing to do with Tatsuha's mouth.

"Where are you, Yuki?" he moaned, tears falling again. Then he turned and looked at Tatsuha accusingly.

Even in a situation like this, all Tatsuha could think about was chasing after the man he loved. In that, he and Shuichi were similar.

"Your own brother's missing," Shuichi shouted bitterly, "and you aren't even worried?!"

"Just because you don't know where he is doesn't mean he's *missing*," Hiro pointed out. "I don't know where *my* brother is at the moment. Should I be worried?"

"Shuichi," Suguru added, "it's not like you report your exact location to your sister every hour of every day."

"True," Shuichi said.

"May I get through?" A sophisticated voice spoke just as Shuichi was about to collapse in a pile of tears. A black-haired girl dressed in a kimono (looking like the romantic ideal of the Taisei era) glared down at Shuichi. She was Ayaka Usami, the daughter of a wealthy Kyoto family. She had once been engaged to Yuki, but was now in a long-distance relationship with Hiro.

"Ayaka!" Hiro cried, stepping on his partner in his rush to reach her. He'd been unable to get in touch with her since she hung up on him at the Ebisu Bridge. Shuichi had run his phone's battery dry, and Hiro had left the charger at the hotel. He'd tried calling from pay phones, but each time, her servants had stated flatly that she wasn't home. He thought that she was so angry at him that she was pretending to be out. So while he had been consoling his hopeless partner, he had also been consoling himself. "You came!"

"Well, I *did* promise." She gave him a flawless smile.

Flustered, Hiro's words caught in his throat. "Uh, um . . . earlier, that was all just him." He pointed at Shuichi.

"Don't worry about it."

"Really?" Hiro said, looking up hopefully. But once he saw her expression, he froze.

"You have nothing to worry about, Hiro Nakano, since you so clearly declared to the entire country that you *don't* currently have a girlfriend."

"Oh, crap. You heard the radio show?" He *had* said that no one in Bad Luck had a girlfriend.

Ayaka nodded coldly.

"Oh! That was . . . um, I mean, we . . ." He was tongue-tied. He hadn't been sure if he could really call her his girlfriend.

"So at the Ebisu Bridge, you declared your love for Shuichi," she said. "It's all becoming very clear now."

Hiro's eyes bugged out. "How'd you figure that?"

"It was on TV. You know, it's very disturbing that I see you more often on TV than I do in person."

"Um . . . Oh, Ayaka, I . . ."

"You *what?*" she asked sharply, unnervingly calm.

Hiro had no idea what to say to get back on her good side. It seemed the more he tried, the deeper a hole he dug. He quickly dissolved into helpless fidgeting, putting on and taking off his hairband, shifting from one foot to the other on top of Shuichi.

Meanwhile, Tatsuha was busy poking Shuichi insistently, making no effort to help him get out from under Hiro's feet.

"Come on, Shuichi," Tatsuha said. "Take me to my dear sweet Ryuichi!" The priest frowned. "You promised to give me some time alone with him!"

"Only after I get some time alone with Yuki!" Shuichi declared.

"Like I care about *that.*"

"I told you on the phone!" Shuichi leapt up, tripping his partner. He stalked off.

"Whoa!" Hiro fell toward Ayaka but managed to brace his hands against the wall and avoid a collision.

"Sorry," Hiro said.

Ayaka was just inches from him, her cheeks flushed a slight pink. "Gosh, you're so pretty."

"Thank you," she murmured.

Hiro laughed. "I know it's a little early, but would you like to visit a shrine with me on New Year's? It'd be great if you wore a kimono then, too."

"So you only want me for my kimono?" She batted her eyes.

"No, not at all! What I meant was . . . If I can see you, then . . ." Flustered, Hiro had completely forgotten that everyone was watching.

Looking up at him, Ayaka suddenly smiled. "Okay then, if we visit a shrine, I'll wear a kimono."

"Really?"

Rolling his eyes, Shuichi stalked off to his waiting room.

"I have a kimono with a sapphire *obi* clasp I think you'd like."

"Wow! With your picture on the cover, our CD sales will shoot through the roof!" Hiro felt emboldened and started to take things too quickly. "We'll cross-promote and sell them everywhere, so . . . if you'd be willing, maybe we should—"

"Ah, Ayaka, how have you been?" A friendly voice disrupted Hiro's perilous proposal. The voice belonged to Tohma Seguchi, president of N-G Pro. He walked in and winked.

Ayaka bowed her head politely and moved quietly away from Hiro.

"We've got twenty or thirty minutes 'til the show begins, so why don't the two of you take a walk in the park?" Tohma suggested.

She nodded. "All right. Come on, Hiro."

"Sure," Hiro assented, worn out from all the upheaval.

"I still have some work to do, so if you'll excuse me," Tohma said, giving them all an angelic smile before heading into the next room.

As Hiro and Ayaka walked out, Ryuichi banged through the door as if propelled by the force of a small explosion. "Hey!" Ryuichi cried, "Shuichi?"

"Like a moth to flame! A feast set before me!" Tatsuha spread his arms. "Ryuichi Sakuma! Your Tatsuha Uesugi is here!"

"Oh, Tatsuha." Ryuichi blinked adorably. "Where's Shuichi?"

There was a slight twitch in Tatsuha's cheek, but he didn't falter. "He had some trouble with my brother and burned out."

Shuichi had left the room to recuperate before the show.

"You've got plenty of time left, don't you? You wanna take a break with me?" Tatsuha winked. "Go somewhere else?"

"I never have to take a break," Ryuichi said. "I can sing forever!"

"I know a place with karaoke," Tatsuha whispered in Ryuichi's ear, wrapping an arm around the young man's slight shoulders. Ulterior motives lurked behind his gentle smile.

Tatsuha was planning a way to take Ryuichi home, and it had almost worked, but Tohma suddenly called out from the next room, "Ryuichi! Did I tell you about the surprise we have planned for today?"

"Surprise?! What kind of surprise?" Ryuichi asked, overjoyed. "Do I get to sing a lot?" He dashed excitedly out of the room. Tatsuha waved helplessly after him. In a split second, Tatsuha's prey had vanished into Nittle Grasper's waiting room. The door was guarded by two men; one resembled a pro wrestler and the other looked like a gorilla.

"Next time I'll make you mine, Ryuichi," Tatsuha vowed, sniggering like a villain who didn't know his days were numbered. He poked his head into Bad Luck's waiting room one more time. "See you next time, Shuichi! And you better make sure Ryuichi and I can be alone, okay?"

The door slammed shut, but no one even noticed.

When the curtain opened on Bad Luck's first Osaka performance, Shuichi was at full throttle, just as he had promised Yuki. Shuichi had reserved a box seat for Yuki on the off chance that he'd come, but the seat remained empty. Still, Shuichi pictured his beautiful lover sitting there; his powerful imagination kept his energy up during the concert, and he was able to sing as powerfully as ever. The fans went wild, unaware that Shuichi was performing his love songs not for them, but for his imaginary Yuki. Even Hiro and Suguru were swept up in the explosive energy that Shuichi created.

"Is this really a good idea?" Suguru mumbled with trepidation, watching Shuichi fling himself a hundred and ten percent into every number.

"Who cares, as long as the tour succeeds?" Hiro replied.

"I guess. As long as he doesn't say anything crazy."

Then the moment they both feared arrived. Panting after running around the stage, Shuichi turned to the audience and started to babble.

"Everyone! Thank you all for coming! I'm so happy to be here! Are you happy to be here?" There was a great cheer. He waited for it to die down before continuing. "Anyone hear the radio show last night?"

"Yes!" almost everyone in the audience shouted.

Watching in the wings, Sakano's face drained of color. "In the name of all that is holy, *please* don't say anything about Yuki!"

"Ah, who cares?!" K said, standing beside Sakano. But Shuichi didn't say anything else.

In an exceedingly rare move, the singer stopped babbling and concentrated on their music. That got the audience even more keyed up.

"I guess we misjudged the power of Shuichi's love," K said.

Sakano nodded in agreement.

Shuichi had decided that the only way to honor the pain Yuki must be feeling during their separation was to stay strong and throw himself into his work. He sang as if life and limb depended on it. As if doing so would help him see Yuki again. There was a violent passion in his voice that had never been there before.

Hiro and Suguru were spurred on by this passion, playing far better than they'd ever thought they could. They forgot their worries and were caught up in the excitement of the performance. Light reflected off their sweat-drenched skin, making them shine. Their energy projected onto the audience, galvanizing each and every fan in the hall.

It was truly amazing.

As the members of Bad Luck neared the end of their greatest performance ever and launched into their final song, Shuichi saw something move in his peripheral vision. *A really late arrival?* Someone was inching toward Yuki's seat. It was a woman dressed up in frills and lace.

It always made him happy when people put a lot of effort into looking good for a show. *That's probably why she's so late. Guess it would take some time making your hair up in rolls like a manga character and covering yourself in gorgeous ribbons. And all those frills on that dress—you can't get on a crowded train, can you, when you're so dressed up?*

In mid-song, even as he looked down at the audience with a broad smile, Shuichi's mind froze.

Dressed up!

When the vocals cut out, Hiro and Suguru looked toward him in surprise.

"You!" Shuichi screamed as he dived off the stage toward the dressed up woman. He leapt toward the seat he had saved for Yuki.

"Why are you sitting here?" he shouted. "What have you done with my Yuki?"

"Your Yuki? Oh, heavens." The woman turned her face away, unable to bear it. Several second passed, and then she slapped Shuichi in the face.

"Ow!" he screamed.

What's that smell . . . ?

Shuichi had smelled it before. As his mind raced, the woman spoke bashfully.

"Oh, thank you for the autograph yesterday."

The memory flooded back. *Right! It's that girl, Seiren. I signed her stocking on the train heading back to Tokyo. And then she ripped my hair out.*

"After that . . ." she started to say hesitantly, but Shuichi wasn't listening.

He began to put things together. The rose scent he'd smelled on the stocking was the same perfume that came from the letter he'd found in Yuki's office.

He began to sniff her all over like a dog searching for smuggled drugs.

"It's you!" Shuichi's keen sense of smell found the scent of his lover on her, despite the smoky air in the hall. "Kunoichi?"

"Yes," she said happily, blushing.

When he saw this, Shuichi boiled over with anger. He completely lost sight of the fact that he was in the middle of a concert.

"How dare you come here to gloat!" he yelled. "Who the hell are you? What did you do with him?" Unable to decide where to grab amongst the frills, he grabbed her rolls of hair and shook them. But before she could say anything, fans stretched out their hands and started touching Shuichi.

"Hey! Stop! Help!" The hands grabbed him all over, and K had to leap into the audience and brandish his machine gun in order to return Shuichi to the safety of the stage.

"Yuki!" his voice carried into the mike, drawing a roar of applause before the curtain dropped on the performance.

It seemed that the audience had mistaken the ruckus for part of the performance. Bad Luck's fans expected unpredictable behavior. In fact, Shuichi's unpredictability was one of the band's best assets.

As soon as the performance ended, Shuichi vanished from the changing room. At the same time, Seiren was busy buying a pile of limited-edition merchandise in the gift shop. She attracted a lot of attention. Many of Bad Luck's fans had made an effort to dress nicely, but no one had gone quite as far as she did.

A tiny guy wearing dark clothes and a pair of sunglasses was sneaking around behind her like a giant cockroach, and walking behind him was a large American with a gun. Everyone instantly recognized Shuichi and K, despite their efforts at disguises. The fans all assumed this was an extension of the evening's show, so they watched quietly. Shuichi was able to follow Seiren around for several minutes, but he lost sight of her the moment she left the hall.

"Where have you taken Yuki?!" Shuichi cried, racing through the crowds blindly, searching for the woman in frills and lace. "Damn you, Kunoichi! I won't give up so easily! I'll get Yuki back from you if it's the last thing I do!"

"Wait, Shuichi!" K shouted, but it was too late. Shuichi had already slipped away through the crowd.

Later that evening, Hiro stood alone outside the Osaka Castle Hall. His stomach growled so loudly that it echoed through the park. K had lost Shuichi, and everyone had split up to search for him.

"Yeah! I never ate dinner," Hiro remembered. He headed for the only dumpling stand that was still open.

"I'll have one of those." Hiro held out a thousand yen bill, keeping his back to the stand. He was afraid that, just like in a movie, the person he was looking for would run by while his back was turned.

"Coming right up! We always use the best ten-legged octopus!"

"Ten legs? Are they genetically altered? I guess there's more to eat if there are extra tentacle?" Hiro

said. His face was still turned toward the street, keeping an eye on the passersby.

"Ah, right! Octopuses have eight legs!"

Hiro sighed. "Everyone knows that."

"Right you are, Hiroshi," the stall keeper said, holding out the tray. Hiro stared at him, astonished.

It was his brother, Yuji. He'd thought the voice was affected, and the Kansai dialect a little fake, but he was bowled over to find his own brother serving him dumplings.

"What the hell are you doing here?" Hiro asked.

"Selling dumplings."

"Yeah, but why are you doing it in *Osaka?*" Hiro asked patiently. He knew that the reason he was able to keep up with Shuichi was thanks to all training he'd had growing up around his senseless big brother.

"My theater troupe's on a sort of freewheeling tour." Yuji laughed heartily. "We filled a van with costumes, backdrops, and actors, and are performing in elementary school auditoriums. But we ran out of money and had to get temp jobs." He sounded awfully happy telling such a dismal tale. "I saw you, Hiro."

"Saw what?"

"You and Ayaka, sitting in a tree, K-I-S-S—"

"What? How?"

"—I-N-G. I've been here all day long, man!"

True enough, Hiro and Ayaka had used the few minutes before the show to take a quick stroll through the park. They'd bought some bird food and fed the pigeons. Hiro had gazed at Ayaka as she watched the birds fight over the seeds. She'd appeared to be having so much fun, but now he felt like they'd done nothing. They hadn't even held hands!

"Embarrassing, huh?"

"Well, I barely saw anything." Yuji laughed. He had the same smile as Hiro. "There were a few girls around that were fans of yours. I talked to them and kept feeding them to keep their attention off you guys. I think I set a new record for dumpling sales!" he said proudly. "You ought to be more aggressive, though." He slapped Hiro on the back. "Just go for it!"

"So how long are you going be selling takoyaki and doing shows at schools?" Hiro asked.

He wanted very badly for his brother to achieve his dreams. Bad Luck had become a major band, so Hiro thought his brother should've been able to parlay that into a part on TV already. Even though Yuji wasn't a schemer, by now it ought to have been happening for him automatically.

"Being a slacker suits you," Hiro said, trying to prod him a little, but all his brother did was grin.

"I just can't give this up!" he said, flipping the dumplings with a practiced rhythm. "I'm having too much fun."

"With takoyaki?"

"Nah. I mean the vibe of it, you know?"

Again, Hiro felt like he was dealing with Shuichi.

"I mean the way we all do everything, put on the play together just like we did in drama club at school. We talk about chasing our dreams and all, and this way it feels like I am. I'm inching toward it!"

"Well, as long as you're happy," Hiro said.

"But seriously, it is a little rough," Yuji admitted, scooping a dumpling onto a tray.

"Seaweed and lots of sauce."

"Pink ginger for free!" Yuji said, plunking a huge mound of the stuff with childlike exuberance. "You know, I don't want to give up the freedom I have."

About to swipe a dumpling off the fryer, Hiro's hand froze. He listened carefully.

"I don't want to give up my stress-free life. If I got paid for acting, I'd probably get a lot of good parts, but it wouldn't be the same. I'd feel trapped. I know people who get too much work and never get to perform in front of a live audience anymore."

To gain one thing often meant losing something else.

Yuji's sentiments took Hiro by surprise. There had certainly been times when the idea of selling out made Hiro cringe, but, in reality, he and Shuichi had lost absolutely nothing. Far from it. They'd gained a lot: Suguru, a producer, a manager, and the chance to work with not only musicians from their own label but all kinds of talented performers.

"That's a limited way of looking at it," Hiro said.

"Yeah, maybe," Yuji replied. "I think you're just stronger than me. I'm afraid to lose anything. I'm scared of change—negative *and* positive—so I guess I do things to keep success in the distant future."

Hiro looked at his brother intently. His words sounded hollow, but his face shone with an enviable ease. He remembered wanting to imitate his brother all the time when he was young, trying to go to kindergarten with him, trying to follow him to elementary school. Then in elementary school he'd met Shuichi, and in junior high they'd started their band. In high school, they finally got some gigs, and then they made their professional debut just after graduation.

"We're all scared of change," Hiro said.

Every time Hiro had tried to support his brother, *he* had been the one who ended up changing. Still, he'd never been in a situation where everything was up to him. He was in love with Ayaka; it was the first time he'd ever been in love. But moving things forward was his responsibility.

"But I'm happy," his brother said, swearing allegiance to his own desires, ignoring the thorns that lined the primrose path. "This time I've got to reach out and grab it with my own hands, even if I get beat up for it."

"I know what you mean!" Hiro agreed. "I've got to kick myself out of this comfortable rut and light a fire under my own butt!"

Both of them reflected a moment on their dreams, smiling quietly.

"Okay," Hiro said. "I gotta go."

"Good luck!" His brother handed over a plastic bag. Hiro took the bag and understood what it implied. There was no need to rush into a decision or a promise. Sometimes words and actions were enough to communicate feelings.

"I can do it when I put my mind to it. Don't worry about me."

"I never worry about you, Hiro. You've always got your stuff together."

Hiro grinned, waved, and turned to leave.

"Is all that for Yuki, then?"

Hiro spun around at this unexpected phrase.

"Yuki? By 'Yuki' you mean Eiri Yuki?"

Not quite picking up on the shock in his voice, Hiro's brother replied casually, "Sure. A little after you and Ayaka went by, someone came to pick some up for him."

"Who was it? Did you get their name and number?"

"Hey, man. I don't pick girls up when I'm working!"

"No, not that . . . Where did she go? We're trying to figure out which hotel Yuki's staying at!"

"Nobody tells the takoyaki man what hotel they're staying at. But it must be close. You know, she sure wore a lot of frills . . ."

"Frills! Please try to remember!" Hiro pleaded. "Something she had with her, anything that might be a clue!"

His brother thought long and hard. He thought so hard he didn't notice all the dumplings burning.

"Oh yeah!" he said, apparently remembering something. Meanwhile, Hiro had started flipping the dumplings and stuffing them onto trays. "She was talking on her cell phone. She said something about seeing Billy Ken tomorrow."

"Billy Ken?"

"You don't know Billy Ken?!" his brother asked, shocked, as if everyone knew him. He was so shocked that Hiro just pretended he did.

"Of course! I was just checking. Okay." He gave a hollow laugh before fleeing.

Watching him leave, his brother murmured, "If someone like Hiro didn't know, then I wouldn't feel ashamed . . . but I guess everyone does. Ah, I'm pathetic!" Still, his mellow Nakano blood soon had him smiling happily as he turned his attention back to the food.

"Billy Ken?" Suguru asked when Hiro returned to the dressing room. Everyone but Shuichi was in the room. "Sounds familiar," the keyboardist said, folding his arms and searching his memory. "But from where?"

"Maybe he's an American," Sakano suggested cheerily.

All eyes turned toward the only American in the room, sitting at a desk with his laptop.

"Billiken is a pointy-headed god of luck," K said.

Everyone was confused. Was he joking?

K gazed into the distance. "Billiken was in a classic movie, so a lot of people know about it."

K's wife was a Hollywood star, so she was constantly talking about movies. He explained that Billiken was a squat, dumpy figure with a mischievous smile and a pointy head. Created by an American sculptor in 1908, the bizarre statue became quite a hit in the 1910s and '20s in both the United States and Japan, and a shrine was even built in his honor in Osaka's Shinsekai district. For the first time ever, everyone looked at K with respect.

"The movie was about a happy couple, but the lead had to go off to war, so his girlfriend gave him a charm for protection. It was shaped like Billiken. They vowed to get married if he came home, but when she heard he had died, she was devastated. She had no way to support herself, so she had to resort to prostitution . . . But!" K slapped the table dramatically; everyone jumped back. "The man was actually alive and came to find her! The woman said to him, 'I'm not the girl I used to be. If you want me, you'd better pay for it.' "

"You're just making this up now, aren't you?" Hiro asked.

"Or did the man give the charm to *her?* I forgot! This was a black and white movie. I saw it a long time ago."

"I think we have more important things to think about than a movie," Sakano said. He stepped to the computer. Until a second before, the screen had displayed a map of Osaka with a flashing light to indicate Shuichi's whereabouts. But now English text streamed across the screen. Sakano was fluent in English. When he had been

Tohma's manager, he'd often gone overseas and dealt with contracts in English. When he read what was on the screen, he fell silent suddenly.

Hiro carried on, unaware of the look of despair on his producer's face. "So how does this Billiken connect to this doll-girl, and how does she connect to Yuki? It's all a mystery."

"Maybe the statue is just a famous landmark, and they've come to write about it?" Suguru wondered, clearly not the slightest bit interested in Yuki's whereabouts. He flopped over on the bed and began rifling through a guidebook. Suguru wasn't worried about Shuichi because he naively thought that Shuichi would come back on his own when he couldn't find the girl. He reasoned that since Yuki was famous, he must have been staying in a hotel that respected its guests' privacy, so there was little hope Shuichi would actually have any success locating him.

Suguru's rational approach to things left little room for the foibles of human nature. It was similar to Tohma's approach. They were, after all, cousins. They also shared brilliant musical skill and showmanship. However, the main difference between them was that Tohma was the type to manipulate people, but Suguru usually wound up being controlled by others.

"K, you know where Shuichi is, right?" Suguru asked. He was relaxed because he knew about the transmitter wedged between Shuichi's teeth which broadcast his whereabouts anytime and anywhere. When Hiro had come back without him, K had fired up his laptop. He seemed to be using a military satellite that provided so much detail that they could make out people walking along the street.

"K? Let's get him back. Where is he?" Hiro asked, feeling recharged after eating the octopus dumplings. He turned toward Sakano and finally noticed that something was wrong. "Sakano! What's going on?"

Sakano didn't reply. He was completely dazed.

Meanwhile, K was working on his computer with uncharacteristic grimness. "Crap! Too late!" he said, hitting the table hard, as if he'd somehow failed to save the world from nuclear annihilation.

"Too late for *what?*" Hiro asked, despite being fearful of the answer.

"You didn't, like, launch a missile in Shuichi's direction or something, did you?" Suguru whispered, hoping against hope.

"I'm afraid I did," K replied.

Both Hiro and Suguru leapt to their feet as if they'd been struck.

"You what?!" Hiro shouted.

"How could you do something like that? We've got a show tomorrow, and the next day, and every day for weeks!" Suguru yelled, throwing his guidebook at K. It hit him in the face. K averted his eyes.

"Sorry, but in six hours . . ."

"Six hours?" Suguru yelled.

"In six hours Osaka will be in flames?!" Sakano screamed.

"How big is the weapon? I've got to call Ayaka and tell her to escape!" Hiro plucked his phone off the charger.

Suguru snatched it from him. "First we've got to call the police and the mayor's office to tell them to evacuate the city!"

"Right, we can't let innocent bystanders get mixed up in this!" Hiro agreed.

BANG! A bullet pierced the phone just as Suguru was about to dial. Both men put their hands up, stepping backward.

Was K about to eliminate the witnesses?

"We won't tell anyone!" Suguru whimpered. "We never saw anything!"

"I just want to live a simple, peaceful life," Hiro pleaded. "Just me and the girl I love!"

"I know you may wish to deny it, but this is really happening," K said apologetically. "For the next six hours, Shuichi will be asleep."

"What? You mean . . ."

"Asleep, or *dead?* Have you suddenly forgotten Japanese?"

K pointed the gun at them, and they went silent. Satisfied, K holstered his weapon, and flopped back down in front of the laptop.

"I've launched my secret weapon at Shuichi."

Suguru and Hiro both bit their tongues, afraid K would whip out his gun again.

"It's a powerful sleeping agent, and though there's some variation, most people are totally knocked out for about six hours. No matter what happens, he won't wake up." An odd smile flashed across K's face. "Behold the power of science!"

Certainly, the idea of Shuichi having randomly fallen asleep somewhere was fraught with danger. A fan might find him and decide to take him home. It was now eleven at night, so he wouldn't wake up until five in the morning. Anything could happen to him.

"And there's a side effect," K said gravely. "Since the body and mind rest perfectly, when he wakes up he will feel incredibly refreshed and filled with energy. He'll be even more hyper than usual."

"That's a side effect?" Hiro asked. "Doesn't sound so bad."

"Well," Suguru said, "with Shuichi that might be very dangerous . . ."

"Ha ha ha! Right! But my point was that after such an energetic day, he'll sleep extremely soundly the next night, so that we can't wake him up!" K laughed.

Timidly, Hiro said, "Well, let's go pick him up. Where is he?"

"Dunno!" K shrugged.

"What do you mean, you don't know?!" Suguru screamed, shaking from stress.

"Well, when I tried to stop the weapon from launching, I cut off the signal. I've been trying to connect again, but I can't seem to do so."

"What, are you using a cheap ISP?" Suguru demanded, his eyes bulging and bloodshot.

"Well, where was he before it went off?" Hiro asked.

"Like I can read *kanji!*" K replied. He started belly-laughing.

Hiro swung his guitar at the blond, but was so upset that he missed.

K finally gave a serious answer. "Actually, when I was trying to stop the tranquilizer missile from homing in on him, I fired off some radio wave disrupters. Even if I do connect to the satellite, I'll have to spend hours repairing the damage before we can find him. But don't worry, I'm sure Shuichi will pull out of it alive."

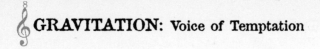

K's words, of course, simply made them worry more, but all they could do was hope that Shuichi was all right.

Track Three:
The Tsutenkaku Tower
Flows with Tears!

The next morning, Shuichi crept quietly into his hotel room near the Osaka Castle.

"Good morning," Shuichi whispered, looking as if he'd just woken up. He was sharing the room with Hiro. He headed toward the bed that didn't have long hair flowing across the pillowcase.

"I'm not sleepy at all." He sniffed under his arms. "Maybe I should shower and get dressed."

Hiro suddenly sat up. His face broke out into a happy, relieved grin. "Shuichi! You're alive!" His eyes were baggy with fatigue, and his hair was a tangled mass.

"Ah, sorry. It's still early. Did I wake you up?"

Hiro shook his head.

"Oh, you were already up?" Shuichi asked.

He shook his head again.

"We haven't been to sleep yet!" Suguru's voice came from the other bed.

Shuichi jumped, startled.

Suguru pushed the blanket aside and sat up in Shuichi's bed. He usually looked deceptively young, but staying up all night had made him look like an old man.

Shuichi noticed that Sakano was kneeling between the two beds, hands together like Buddha. Over on the windowsill, K sat clutching his rifle like a soldier in the trenches.

"Um, did you guys wait up all night?"

All of them nodded gravely. Their sunken, bloodshot eyes glared at him, piercing Shuichi's heart.

"Sorry! I meant to come back, but . . ."

Shuichi had plunged into the crowds outside the Osaka Castle Hall looking for Seiren. He had found himself caught up in the throng of people, pushed along by the mass of tourists and concertgoers heading toward the Osaka Castle Station, and before he knew it, he was on the loop line. He was swept along by the crowd again, right out of the ticket gates at some other station. Since he'd chased Seiren right after the show, he didn't have his wallet or his phone with him.

"I tried to figure out a way back," Shuichi told them. "But the farther I went, the more lost I got. I was totally in the middle of nowhere, and it was dark! And I could hear wild animals growling! Wild, bloodthirsty animals looking for their next meal!"

"Wild animals?" Hiro asked incredulously.

"You mean stray dogs?" Suguru asked, just as skeptical as Hiro.

Shuichi hugged himself, shaking at the memory. "I was so scared! I thought I was going to be eaten by a lion, and I'd never get to see Yuki ever again! But, you know, the weirdest thing happened—I don't know if it was my fear or what, but I fell asleep in the middle of the street!"

Shuichi got more and more excited as he went on, but no one could follow what he was saying. "Next thing I know, I woke up to find myself surrounded by cardboard boxes and newspapers. I guess some nice people saw that I was asleep and took care of me so I wouldn't catch a cold. I actually slept great! I feel revved up! I could climb Mount Everest!"

"Well, at least *you* got to sleep." Hiro collapsed back on the bed.

"And the drug's side effect is exactly what K said it would be." Suguru yawned, retreating back under the covers. He muttered something about wanting a dose of it himself, but it was muffled under the layers of blankets.

"What?" Shuichi asked. "What did K do this time?"

Sakano was carrying a teapot across the room when K's shoulders stiffened and the rifle he'd been about to put back in its case slipped from his fingers. The heavy barrel landed right on Sakano's foot.

"Ow!" the producer cried, toppling over backward, teapot and all. Hot tea splashed all over the carpet. He took a moment to recover, then said, "Well, as long as Shuichi is safe." A few tears rolled down his cheeks. "All's well that ends well."

"Sorry, everybody!" Shuichi announced cutely. "While I'm apologizing I might as well let you know! I'm off to find Yuki now!"

Shuichi expected to hear violent objections, but the room was deathly quiet. The lack of reaction actually scared him more. He wondered if everyone was asleep, so he tried again.

"Um, so, I'm going to look for Yuki, okay?"

"Suit yourself," Suguru said. "But do you actually know where he is?"

"I don't think you're going to find him just searching randomly," Hiro said.

With the utmost confidence, Shuichi waved them off. "When love's involved, miracles happen all the time!"

Shuichi beamed at them; K patted him on the head as if he were a puppy. "That's the spirit, Shuichi! Here, fetch!" He threw a book all the way across the room.

"I'm not a dog!" Shuichi grumbled, running after the book anyway. He felt like he'd find Yuki soon, so he was in a very good mood as he checked the bookmarked page. It was a map of Tennoji, the historic district of Osaka. He turned to everyone, pointing to a photograph of the Tsutenkaku Tower, and shouted, "This! When I woke up, I saw this!"

Oblivious to the mood in the room, he glanced quickly over the rest of the page. "I saw this too!" Finally he understood. "I get it. I could hear wild animals 'cause I was right next to the zoo!" He laughed cheerfully.

"You know, Yuki's going to see Billiken tomorrow," Hiro said. "Which I guess would be today, now."

Shuichi brightened. "Billy Ken? Then I'll go meet this Billy Ken dude too!"

"Billiken's not a person, he's a god. He's enshrined at Tsutenkaku."

"Here?" Shuichi looked closely at the picture, tears welling up in his eyes. They sparkled. Everyone just stared at him.

They knew exactly what Shuichi would say.

"Yuki! Our love made a miracle! Our love drew me to you! But I was a fool!" He pounded his fist on the bed, forgetting that Suguru was lying there. "If I had just waited, you would've found me! I'm coming back, Yuki! Wait for me!"

Since Shuichi appeared ready to dive out the window, the others had to hold him down. Eventually, after having some sense talked into him, Shuichi agreed to wait until the tower was open. They would all go together after everyone had gotten some sleep.

"Okay, okay, I understand. You all want to witness our miraculous reunion. But you know, when the two of us get together, anything could happen. So be sure you just say hi then leave, okay?" He giggled, looking utterly love-struck, but no one was paying attention. They were already fast asleep.

Only K managed to stay awake long enough to set up a heavy-duty smoke bomb on the door to protect his clients. "Don't try to open the door until I disconnect this, okay? Or it'll explode.

Good night!" And in an instant, he too was fast asleep, snoring loudly.

Shuichi did his best to be patient.

"Yuki will be listening tonight, so I'd better rehearse!"

Because he'd slept so soundly, he sang loud enough to shake the walls and rattle the windows. A seemingly endless number of phone calls came in, complaining about the noise. Hiro, Suguru, and Sakano got no sleep at all. Only K slept soundly, his battle-hardened ears immune to such disturbances.

An arcade lined with gift shops, restaurants, and *pachinko* parlors led up to the landmark Tsutenkaku Tower. There were strange, giant blowfish adorning the shop signs, but Shuichi didn't notice them. He ran straight down the center of the cobblestones.

"Yuki! *Je t'aime!*" he shouted in French, the language of love, perhaps inspired by the fact that the Tsutenkaku Tower looked like a miniature Eiffel Tower.

"Billiken's up there," K said, pointing to the glassed-in observation deck six stories up.

"So is Yuki!" Shuichi shouted.

"Well, to get to the observation deck we'll have to pay for an elevator ride," Hiro said.

"Once I get there, I can see Yuki!"

"Gosh, it's pretty expensive," Sakano said. "I wonder if the expense accounts will cover it."

"Look how tall it is! If we make out up there, everyone in Osaka will be able to see us!" Shuichi exclaimed.

"Or no one. Because you'll look as small as ants," Suguru said, but Shuichi was too wrapped up in his own fantasy to hear.

"Aha! That's Yuki!" Shuichi screamed, seeing someone on the observation deck who appeared as tiny as a grain of rice. His love was not about to be conquered by mere distance. He started running, propelled by his fierce longing. "I found him!"

"Shuichi! Wait!"

He ran ahead toward Tsutenkaku, unable to wait any longer. Hiro, Suguru, and Sakano trailed after him like three braindead zombies.

"Yuuukiii!" He rushed into the tower entrance. He zipped past the crowd of people trying to get on the elevator and headed for the spiral staircase inside. He was up all six flights in no time. It never occurred to him that Yuki might take the elevator down while he was running up. He was sure Yuki would wait for him.

Shuichi burst out the door at the top of the stairs. A gift shop lady got in his way and tried to say something to him, but he zipped around her like the wind past a tree.

Without paying for a ticket, he sped past all the people waiting in line and dove into the observation deck elevator just as it was leaving. He didn't notice the look of consternation the elevator attendant gave him. None of the other passengers said a word. They didn't have the courage to oppose a man who looked so determined.

When the elevator reached the observation deck, Shuichi jumped out. The glass walls afforded

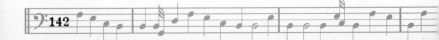

a beautiful view of the city, but he didn't so much as spare it a glance. He found himself reeling from the lack of oxygen. Even with his powerful lungs, running all the way up had made him breathless.

"Yuki? Yuki?!" he panted, doubled over, trying to catch his breath. Just then, he caught a beloved scent in the air. It was a smell no normal person would ever notice, but it grabbed Shuichi and wouldn't let go. *It's Yuki's essence.*

He turned and saw Yuki standing there.

"Shuichi?" Yuki said, looking at him with surprise. His cold, beautiful face was a shade less guarded than usual. There seemed to be warmth lurking beneath the ever-present chill.

Maybe it's just an illusion, simple wish fulfillment. No, he loves me!

"Oh, Yuki!" Pearl-sized tears dripped out of Shuichi's eyes. He hurtled toward his lover, as if shot from a catapult, with his arms spread wide, ready for a hug. "I found you! I missed you!"

But before he got there, Shuichi tripped, tumbling head over heels.

"What the hell are you doing?" Yuki said.

Oh! He's standing right here in front of me! He's looking at me and talking to me!

The familiar face that looked down at him from a slight distance was intolerably beautiful. There was a trace of annoyance in Yuki's eyes, but the length of his separation from the novelist made even this expression seem beautiful.

"Yuuukiiii!" he cried, getting up and plunging into his lover's chest before collapsing again onto the floor. His tears kept flowing, but he started to giggle. Everyone who had been looking out over the streets of Osaka turned and crowded around Shuichi.

Yuki stood still, making no effort to run away. Some witnesses later told the gossip rags that he looked like a mother protecting her fallen child. Others said he looked like a deer caught in headlights, or a man frozen by the sight of some unspeakable horror.

"Oh! Yuki, it was awful!" The longed-for rhythm of Yuki's heartbeat synchronized with his own, and he felt lost in emotion.

"How did you find me?" Yuki asked.

"Through the force of our love!" Shuichi said proudly, looking up, arms still wrapped tightly around his lover.

Yuki looked exactly the same as he always did: slightly irritated.

Would it kill him to coo, "Oh, Shuichi, I've been longing for you!" or something? Well, knowing him it probably would. It would be so nice, though. But Yuki is Yuki. He isn't going to change just because we're in Osaka.

"I was *so* worried!" Shuichi whined plaintively. "You weren't at home, and you didn't answer the phone, and there was a weird letter, and I didn't know where you were!"

Still, Yuki's expression didn't change. Shuichi started to worry. He wanted to ask so many questions.

Why did you leave without me? You could have at least said something. But he kept silent. Anyway, the sight of Yuki's face made those anxieties melt away.

Shuichi reached his hands up to touch his lover's cheek.

SMACK! Yuki slapped Shuichi's hand away. Ignoring this token resistance, Shuichi got up and pressed his lips onto Yuki's.

"Get off!" Yuki said, shoving Shuichi away, then kicking him as hard as he could.

Shuichi's tiny body flew all the way back to the arcade and slammed into a pinball machine in the corner. "Unh!"

He hit it so hard it let out a metallic wheeze before all its lights shut off. But the tremble that ran through Shuichi's body wasn't caused by pain. He stood up, a few drops of blood dripping from his nose.

"Don't be so embarrassed!" Shuichi said, walking forward, dragging his left leg behind him like a zombie. "Tatsuha told me they had you locked up in some hotel."

For each lurching step Shuichi took closer, his lover took one back. There was a tension in the air never before experienced at a happy tourist trap like Tsutenkaku.

Suddenly, Shuichi felt someone's eyes on him. He spun around. Seiren, the woman who dressed like a baby doll, was glaring at him. *She's the girl who demanded my autograph and tore out my hair on the train. She's the woman who took the seat reserved for Yuki at the concert. And so she has to be the lady editor who kidnapped Yuki and held him captive!*

"So it *was* you!" Shuichi growled, glaring back at her, not to be outdone.

"Ah!" Seiren writhed, her tightly curled hair shaking.

"Let's go," Yuki said, laying a hand on her shoulder and walking away.

"Yuki? Yuki! Where are you going?" Shuichi ran after them.

"Away from you," Yuki said, ripping his lover's heart into shreds. Yuki turned back to Shuichi to reveal his long, narrow eyes, now seething, colder and angrier than ever before.

"Why?" Shuichi stood in shock. *Is he angry with me because I didn't answer his call?*

"You should probably know," Seiren said as she turned around. "I'm Yuki's—"

"Don't tell him," Yuki snapped.

She had sounded oddly happy. Something was going on between them, something Shuichi didn't know about.

"You don't mean—Yuki! You and that . . . that woman!"

"Go away," Yuki hissed. Yuki was . . . rejecting him. "Never show yourself before us again."

"Oh, don't be so mean to Shuichi!" Seiren said.

"Silence," Yuki insisted.

Shuichi stood aghast as Yuki turned his back and began walking toward the elevator. *What's going on?*

"Hey! Wait!" Shuichi chased after him but was a few steps too slow. Just as he reached the doors of the elevator, they closed in his face.

"Ow!" He slammed straight into them. But he wasn't going to lose Yuki again because of some elevator. He raced down the stairs almost as fast as the elevator descended.

"Yuki!" he screamed on his way down.

He crashed into Suguru and Hiro, who had been on their way up. Even *that* didn't stop him. They screamed as they all fell down the spiral staircase together, the centrifugal force causing them to roll faster and faster.

They protested loudly, but Shuichi just kept shouting, "Yuki!"

THUMP! THUMP! THUMP!

Like a trio of donuts, they rolled all the way to ground floor. It was filled with tourists and locals who'd come running when they heard the ruckus.

"Are you okay?" Sakano asked. "Is everyone alive?"

"I think so," Suguru said, untangling himself and standing up.

Shuichi was left on the floor, squished like a pancake.

"Shuichi, speak to me!" Hiro shook him.

"I can't." Every inch of his body hurt, but it was his heart that ached the most.

"Oh, heavens! Somebody, call a doctor! Help! Ambulance!" Sakano whipped out his cell but was much too panicked to dial, so he started to hit himself in the head with it over and over again.

The tourists just stared, shocked.

"There'll be a helicopter here in less than five minutes," K growled after pulling out his walkie-talkie.

"Don't bother," Shuichi announced. "I'm okay!"

Hiro breathed a sigh of relief. "Shuichi says he's okay."

"But surely you broke all your bones," Sakano wailed.

"Just leave me alone!" Shuichi yelled, his bottled-up fury silencing the murmuring crowd. "I need to be alone!"

"Well, if that's what you need," K said, "as your manager, I'll massacre everyone in here."

Ignoring K, Suguru said calmly, "Hard to leave you alone here in a public place. In fact your lying here is probably a public nuisance."

Sakano hyperventilated. "How is he ever going to perform tonight? How will I ever explain this to Tohma?"

"Yuki doesn't want me anymore," Shuichi moaned.

Upon hearing his faint voice, all the onlookers burst into tears. Standing nearby, a dumpling seller was so moved that he stepped forward and embraced Shuichi.

"Hey, you're Hiro's brother," Shuichi said, blinking in surprise. He felt their artistic souls synchronize.

They flung their arms around each other and sobbed. Everyone else was left confounded.

Sakano took his glasses off and rubbed his nose. "I do feel sorry for Shuichi. We have to help him. We have to get him back together by nightfall." He started to cry.

In Bad Luck's dressing room at the Osaka Castle Hall just minutes before the show, everyone was unexpectedly upbeat.

Sakano was ironing his shirt.

THWACK! At the sudden noise, his hand jerked upward. "Ow! Ow! Ow!" he yelped, after accidentally putting the iron back down on his left hand. He did a wild dance of pain, but nobody paid him the slightest bit of attention.

Shuichi was pounding the television with his fist, shouting, "I'm busy burning down heartbreak hotel! How dare you throw salt in my wounds by refusing to work?!" He pointed his index finger at the television screen and announced, "Only one person gets to give me static!"

Everyone else in the room turned and hit him with their folding fans.

"What on Earth is going on?" Tohma asked as he walked in, changing the channel with the remote. He smiled sharply. "This morning, you altered the schedule without permission to create this ruckus? You really must consult with me first."

There was a severity in his smile that made K tongue-tied. "Oh! Boss, what? I don't speak Japanese well!"

As he laughed, Sakano, Hiro, and Suguru all dropped to their hands and knees. Sakano pulled a strip of paper and a brush from somewhere and began scrawling a farewell haiku.

"I'm not scolding you," Tohma said. "I just want to know what happened."

He glanced back at the television where the newscaster and celebrity beat reporter were speaking excitedly.

"It seems the novelist Eiri Yuki and the lead singer of Bad Luck, Shuichi Shindou, are in Splitsville!"

There was no way for Sakano or N-G Pro to hide the morning's melodramatic love scene and ensuing devastation, since it had happened in front of hundreds of witnesses at the Tsutenkaku Tower.

It was almost instantly on every gossip show. Because it had taken place in Osaka, quite a number of popular comedians had something to say about it.

"I bet it's on in America. CBS, ABC—even the nature channel!" Shuichi wailed, his shoulders slumping.

"Don't worry, Shuichi," Hiro said, plucking the strings of his guitar. "No matter how many awards Yuki's won, unless we've got a chart-topping hit in America, none of them will pay any attention to us."

"Hiroshi couldn't be more right," K said as he greased his beloved magnum. "What you've got to do, Shuichi, is funnel all that pain and heartbreak into your singing. Show your Japanese heart! Sing powerfully all night long!"

"Think of the bright side," Suguru said casually. "At least you two lasted this long and were very happy together. Even a crazy guy like you was able to have an ordinary . . . sort of . . . relationship."

"I'll show him!" Shuichi yelled, his pain morphing into rage. "I'll give the best damn performance of my career. I'll *make* him fall in love with me again!"

"I'm sure this station isn't covering the story," Sakano said, changing the channel to Public Broadcasting in an attempt to soothe Shuichi. But even there, they were covering yesterday's plunge into the Dotonbori River.

"You're kidding!" Shuichi wailed.

The reporter informed the viewers that a musician had leapt into the river after a phone call from his lover. She went on to report that the musician had tried to patch things over at the Tsutenkaku Tower, but had been rejected, and then had fallen down the stairs along with his bandmates.

Something about the reporter's calm, flat monotone set Shuichi off. "Can't you just let me be depressed without reminding me of *why* I'm depressed?!" And again he started beating the unfortunate television set.

"Really, Shuichi, it's your own fault," Tohma said with an unusual stiffness to his normally pleasant voice. It worried everyone. "So it's up to you to fix it."

"Fix it how?" Shuichi said, still gazing at the footage on the screen. He saw himself at the peak of his own bliss, his arms wrapped around Yuki. He was so embarrassingly unguarded. It made for terrible publicity. But he was so obviously happy in those images that he was jealous of himself. He bit his lip. *If only I could rewind the world back to that moment.*

"Put your hands in the air," K said, poking him with a gun. "This is a stickup!"

Shuichi put his hands up, trembling with fear.

"Shuichi! Promise you won't give up, or I'll shoot!" K looked down at him, grinning. "Just a little joke! Actually, I've got some big news for you."

Shuichi sighed. "That never means anything good."

"You'd better listen."

Suddenly the music that marked the beginning of the night's performance began playing, followed by screams from the audience loud enough to shake the waiting room.

Laser beams gleamed across the stage, and images of the band flashed on the giant screens, whipping the audience into a frenzy.

"Starting already?"

"Come on, Shuichi," Hiro said.

"We'll talk later," Suguru added.

"Oh man!" Shuichi moaned, suddenly hit with stage fright. It had been years since he'd felt like this. The last time was when he'd performed a love song he'd written with Yuki in mind. Yuki had come to see him, so Shuichi had wanted to perform his first *real* love song.

My Yuki just walked away. He left me alone! How can I sing?

"You want me to warm them up for you?" a familiar voice asked.

Shuichi looked up. "Ryuichi?"

Ryuichi Sakuma leaned against the door casually. Uncharacteristically, there wasn't a stuffed animal in his hands. In fact, there was no sign at all of his customary childishness. Instead, he stood there confidently, sporting a fearless gaze.

Ever since he'd been a child, Shuichi had admired Ryuichi's ability to put aside all the troubles in his life and devote every ounce of his energy to his performances. It was Ryuichi who had almost single-handedly etched the name Nittle Grasper onto the world's consciousness.

"In the state you're in, you can't sing after me," Ryuichi said.

Ryuichi's words fired Shuichi up, making his anger and sadness disappear.

"Don't be silly!" Shuichi said. "Warm-up's *my* job! But thanks anyway." His energy restored, Shuichi darted out of the waiting room.

K chased after him, shouting, "Wait, Shuichi. I've got big news!"

"Not now! The show's starting!" Shuichi yelled.

Once on the stage, Shuichi was unusually aggressive and passionate. The audience wondered if Bad Luck was finally casting off the shackles of their comedy band label. The concert was a tremendous success . . .

But Shuichi wasn't satisfied. After the show, he turned on his companions the moment they hit the waiting room.

"Tomorrow's the last Osaka show," he said. "Then we're on the road again. My point being, the only night I can spend with Yuki is tonight! So I'm going to see him, no matter what I have to sacrifice! If anyone dares to get in my way, I'll mow you down!"

"Yes, sir!" K said with a salute and started to gear up.

Hiro, Suguru, and Sakano made no move to restrain him.

"I figured out why Yuki was angry!" Shuichi continued. "He tried to call me, but I didn't answer! He's sulking! He's always withdrawn! But all we need to do is talk, and everything will work out!" Despite the public humiliation that morning, despite the shock of being dumped, Shuichi clearly believed that all he had to do was see Yuki again and everything would be forgotten.

"Um, Shuichi." Hiro raised his hand. "How exactly do you plan to find him?" He had clearly given up on his own relationship; he was so close to Kyoto and his girlfriend, but his partner's crisis was keeping them apart.

"Ha ha ha! I thought you might ask!" K said, happily taking out his computer. "I told you I've got news!" He patted his laptop.

"That's not going to do anything," Shuichi said to K. "You already know where *I* am." But then he froze.

The flashing light should have been on Osaka Castle Hall, surrounded by Osaka Castle, the river, and the JR railroad tracks. But that's not what the map showed.

"What's that?"

"Well," K said, blushing, "thanks to your passionate kiss, the location of the transmitter has shifted."

"To Yuki? Seriously?!"

"Surely it's made better than that!" Sakano said. "It wouldn't shift so easily, would it?"

"Yuki must have quite an impressive technique!" Suguru noted.

"Of course he does. But that's none of your business!" Shuichi said, smacking Suguru in the chest, sending him flying back. Suguru crumpled to the floor on top of Sakano, who had already passed out from the force of his nosebleed at the mere suggestion of Yuki's technique.

"Why didn't you tell me *sooner?*" Shuichi demanded. "I could have put even more love into my performance!" Shuichi started pummeling K with his fists.

K drew his gun and pointed it at Shuichi's face. "Excuse me? I kept trying to give you the big news. But no, you were too nervous about the show to listen!"

"Ah! Right. Sorry; all my fault. I'll apologize until my throat bleeds—but later. I need you to take me to Yuki right now!"

And so they made a plan so outrageous, so deranged, that history had never seen its equal.

Track Four:
Operation: Voice of Temptation

Later that evening, a black helicopter flew across the Osaka skyline. It provided a spectacular view of the city lights gleaming in the dusk—a view that would have been perfect for two lovers sharing a romantic flight. But the helicopter was filled with the members of Bad Luck. They wore military clothing provided by K, so they looked more like a special ops force than musicians.

"No other band in the world has to do this while on tour," Suguru complained, his face unusually sallow. He didn't really like heights, and the chopper was making him queasy.

Hiro nodded. He, too, lacked the energy he usually displayed.

Spread out in their laps was a blueprint of the hotel where Yuki was staying. There was even a list detailing when the guards were scheduled to patrol. When asked how he'd been able to get this kind of information, K just winked and smirked, refusing to divulge his source.

"Yuki's in here," Shuichi whispered lovingly, rubbing his finger over a room on the blueprint.

"Target in sight!" K said. "Prepare for descent!"

The helicopter was buffeted by winds that ran up around the building. Suguru hung grimly onto the edge of the open door, watching the target approach, unable to believe his eyes.

"He was here all along?" Hiro asked.

"Wait!" Suguru yelled.

"Too late for that!" K said. "Ready, set, go!"

K shoved Suguru and Hiro out the door before they had a chance to work up the nerve. Next was Shuichi.

"Good luck!" K said, giving him a thumbs-up.

"I'm coming, Yuki!" Shuichi yelled as he leapt out the door all by himself.

Finally K slid down a rope. He carried Sakano on his back.

"President! Please forgive my early departure from this world!" Sakano babbled. "I'm giving my life for the agency! I hope I'll be remembered for my humble sacrifice!" Even before his tearful speech was finished, he was standing safely on the roof of the hotel.

"Is it really *this* hotel?" Suguru asked in disbelief.

"My satellite tracking system is never wrong!" K said.

Shuichi grinned broadly, anticipating his reunion.

"Right in our blind spot," Hiro said. He was certainly glad for his partner's good cheer, but his deeper feelings were bit more complicated. He longed to be with Ayaka.

"This is *our* hotel!" Sakano shrieked, swinging a paper fan wildly. "Why the hell did we take a helicopter? Why did we risk our lives with such a dangerous rooftop landing?"

"It's like a performance!" K beamed. "Now we're all in the right mood. We're more energized and ready to get Yuki back!"

"Hey, everyone!" Shuichi spoke. "Let's work together as friends and bandmates to rescue Yuki from his evil captor! Follow me to victory!"

And with shouts of solidarity, Hiro, Suguru, and Sakano followed Shuichi into the building.

"Do we really need to do this?" Suguru asked, hunched in the hallway corner, a spray can gripped firmly in his hand.

"I don't know," Hiro said from the opposite corner, his long hair tied back in a ponytail. "But we can't stop now."

Hearing quiet footsteps, they both peered carefully down the hall. A somber bellhop was walking toward them, tired from a long day at work. The timing was exactly as K's report had predicted.

"Go!" Hiro yelled.

Hiro and Suguru leapt out and sprayed their cans in the bellboy's face.

PSHHH! Neon pink and yellow silly string sprayed all over the unsuspecting victim.

"Ugh!" he screamed. The wet, rubbery texture must have unnerved him, because he began scratching at his face, frantically trying to get it off.

"Yeah! Par-tay!" Hiro shouted, acting like a drunk guest.

"Strip rock, paper, scissors!" Suguru said, playing along.

The bellboy relaxed and instantly joined in the game.

Naturally, both Hiro and Suguru were extremely good at rock, paper, scissors. Playing their instruments had made their fingers swift and assured. Neither of them would ever get stuck between paper and scissors and wind up sticking out three fingers.

Soon enough, the bellboy was totally naked.

"Here!" Suguru said, handing him a sunflower from one of the vases decorating the hall.

"Um," the poor man said, covering himself.

"Don't worry," Hiro assured him. "We'll bring your clothes back as soon as we're done."

Suguru and Hiro fled, leaving the bellboy hiding his crotch with the sunflower. Too ashamed to go to the staff changing rooms, he hid in the nearest restroom and hoped they'd remember to bring his clothes back.

KNOCK. KNOCK.

Seiren opened the door. She was wearing one of her frilly dresses.

"Your dinner, madam," Suguru said, disguised as a bellhop.

"But we didn't order room service."

"Oh? I do apologize," he said, glancing quickly around the room. He bowed his head. "There must have been some mistake. Please accept this meal, on the house." He walked into the room carrying a tray with a covered dish on it. He placed the tray on the table.

"Thanks, but we're really not hungry," Seiren said.

"Don't worry about it. Enjoy!" Suguru slipped away quickly. Outside, he whispered, "Target confirmed. The bird is in the coop!"

Following instructions from the transmitter attached to his ear, he nodded at Hiro, who was dressed as a maid.

Hiding his face behind a feather duster, Hiro knocked on the door.

"Yes?" Seiren opened the door.

"Here to change the sheets," Hiro said in an odd, high-pitched voice. He quickly pushed a cart covered by a sheet into the room.

"They're clean," Seiren protested. "We really don't need new sheets. Didn't you see the 'Do Not Disturb' sign?" Seiren tried to close the door, but the oversized cart—large enough for a grown man to fit inside—got in the way. She tried again, but Hiro wouldn't budge. She gave up, and he pushed the cart all the way into the room.

"Well, at least be quiet, okay? Don't make a ruckus," the girl warned.

"I can't make any promises," Hiro said in his normal voice, still hiding his face behind the feather duster. "You see, we came specifically to make a ruckus!"

Seiren shrieked, her curly hair shaking. She ran to the far side of the room, where Yuki sat.

"Wh-who are you?" she asked in a trembling voice, wringing her lace handkerchief.

Yuki had been facing away from Hiro. "I've heard that voice before." He glanced quickly over his shoulder but kept his fingers on his laptop's keyboard. "I'm busy!" he shouted at Hiro. "Play your silly little spy games on your own time."

"Well, at least you're being straightforward with me," Hiro said pulling the duster away from his face. "I brought you a package. I hope you'll be straightforward with it, too."

He rolled the cart forward.

Yuki casually lit a cigarette and blew a cloud of smoke into Hiro's face.

"Here we go." Hiro began shaking the sheet that covered the cart. Five . . . Four . . . Three . . . Two . . . One . . ."

Nothing happened. No one came out of the cart. His wide smile gradually faded. He sighed.

Just when Hiro was getting ready to push the cart out of the room, there was a thunderous noise. Shuichi came swinging in from outside the building and crashed through the window, sending shards of broken glass flying everywhere.

Yuki was at a loss for words. He stared, mouth agape.

"All right, Seiren!" Shuichi announced. "I'm here to take my Yuki back!" Breathing hard, Shuichi pointed his index finger at his lover. "You! Why did you lie to me?"

Even Yuki, so used to writing dramatic scenes, was taken aback by this unexpected turn of events. His cigarette had slipped from his fingers and was rolling across the carpet. Still dressed as a cleaning lady, Hiro quickly picked it up.

"Surprised?" Hiro asked cheerfully.

Yuki ignored him and spoke to Shuichi. "What are you doing?"

"It's obvious, isn't it?!" Shuichi cried, glass crunching beneath his feet as he approached.

Yuki had rocked Shuichi to his core at Tsutenkaku. All of Shuichi's expectations—all the things he'd assumed Yuki would do because Yuki really loved him—had suddenly and violently been ripped away from him. All that was left was his love, raw like an open sore.

"I want to see you!" Shuichi replied. "I *need* to see you."

Yuki didn't respond.

"So all you have to do is admit you want to see me too!" Shuichi cried.

Yuki glared back at him.

"I know you're pissed because I didn't answer when you called," Shuichi said. "And I am sorry about that, but . . ."

"I called?"

"Yeah, yesterday. You called my cell, right? K kicked it into the Dotonbori River by accident. I fell in after it, and then we were dragged aboard a submarine. So I couldn't answer."

Yuki cocked his head to the side. "Oh, that's interesting. You can't get a signal inside a submarine? I'll have to remember that for my next book."

"That's not the point!" Shuichi screamed, then dropped to his knees. "I'm sorry! I'm so, so, so sorry!"

Hiro couldn't believe what he was witnessing. Never had he thought that all this trouble was just so Shuichi could make an apology.

Yuki seemed unmoved. "I see," he muttered, glaring at Seiren.

She flinched, wringing her frilly dress.

"That call wasn't from me," Yuki said.

"Huh?" Shuichi looked up at him.

Seiren fell to her knees and bowed. "It was me!" Her curls spilled onto the floor like a mop.

"I'm an editor for Kunoichi Monthly. My code name is Seiren. It's a ninja magazine, so we all use code names! We're skilled in the art of escape, so when I got away from you last night, I never thought you'd be able to find us here."

Shuichi frowned. "I knew you had Yuki locked up, but what I'm talking about is . . ."

"*I* called you yesterday using Yuki's mobile phone," she confessed, her eyes screwed tightly shut. "I took the cell from him."

"What?" Shuichi was lost in a spiral of confusion. *Does she mean like on TV, when a mistress calls a wife and says, "Do you know where your husband is?" Basically announcing that she planned to steal him away for good?*

As he swayed in shock, Suguru, K, and Sakano came into the room. They'd heard every word of the conversation over the transmitter that Hiro carried.

"Why did you do that?" Hiro asked gently, handing a sheet to the teary Seiren.

"Because," Seiren said, glancing at Yuki. "I thought Yuki wanted to see Shuichi."

Everyone stared at Yuki. A quiver passed over his pretty face. "I've had just about enough of this," he said, gathering up his laptop and heading for the next room.

"Yuki!" Shuichi moaned, giving him a desperate look.

"I'm almost done," Yuki said. "Just wait a little longer." He slammed the door behind him.

"He just can't admit it," Shuichi and Seiren said in unison.

Seiren nodded at him apologetically. "I keep telling him to call you and spend some time with you."

"You mean, you're a good guy? You're on my side?" Shuichi brightened.

"I'm such a big fan of both of you, and I want to see you together."

"I wanted to be with him all this time!"

Both of them were still down on their knees, their spirits now in harmony.

"Aha!" Hiro said, slapping his knee.

Everyone finally understood.

"So you wanted to see Yuki and Shuichi together, so you used Yuki's phone to call Shuichi?" Hiro asked.

"That *would* piss Yuki off," Suguru added.

"Yes!" Seiren said. "Mister Yuki is too shy! He never does anything in public with Shuichi."

"So what on Earth have we been doing all this time?" Sakano asked. "All the trouble we've caused Tohma! I don't know how I'll ever make it up to him!" He burst into tears, instantly drenching an entire sheet from the cleaning cart.

"But if that was true, why didn't you say so at the concert?" Shuichi asked.

Seiren looked puzzled. "You didn't know?"

"How could I?"

"But I told your president, Tohma Seguchi," she said.

Everyone in the room looked stunned.

"Tohma?" Shuichi said hesitantly.

And just then, the man himself walked in.

"Yes, me," the president said, grinning as he stood in the doorway that Yuki had just gone through. "After all the trouble I went through to get Yuki in Osaka, you never came. I was starting to wonder what had happened to you."

"Huh?"

Tohma put his finger to his lips. "Or didn't I tell you?"

Shuichi gaped at him hopelessly.

"When you called to tell me Yuki was missing, I asked if you'd looked carefully. Seiren said she left a note for you with all the contact information."

Really? Shuichi's unreliable memory raced backward.

"Yuki seemed reluctant to tell you anything, so I wrote down the name of the hotel, the room number, and the phone number."

"But the note didn't have any of that!" Shuichi insisted.

Seiren tilted her head to the side. "I wrote it on the second page."

"Second page?" He moaned, as if his soul was halfway out of his body. He didn't know there was more to the note.

"I want you two to stay together always!" Seiren's eyes sparkled. She pulled a pair of white lace stockings out of her big, lacy purse. Shuichi had signed one of them on the train. The other one had been signed by Yuki.

"I've placed strands of your hair in each of them!" Seiren giggled. She looked as adorable as a doll, but the way she thought sent a chill down Suguru's spine.

"I guess one stocking is totally useless without the other." Hiro said, understanding the significance of her gesture. "When a sock loses its partner, it loses its purpose. Each sock exists for the other—a pair."

When Hiro's explanation was over, a waterfall of tears flowed down Shuichi's face.

"You thought so highly of us! Thank you! Thank you!" Shuichi pumped Seiren's dainty, laced hand like a victorious politician thanking his supporters at the end of a close election.

I'm so happy! You understand my feelings! Yuki never says anything like that, but if everyone else thinks that's how things are, then who cares?!

Excitement flooded through both of them. Shuichi and Seiren appeared to have very similar personalities. They had connected and no longer needed words to understand each other.

"Glad this makes you happy," Tohma said.

Despite having been tricked, teased, and toyed with, Shuichi held out his hand. "Thanks, Tohma! Thanks for everything."

"Thank *you*. Your performances the last two nights have been outstanding. I'm very satisfied. Osaka can be a bit of a turning point, you see. I was worried you'd hit a slump, but there was a splendid edge to it." He smiled angelically. "Honestly, it's been quite awhile since I had this much fun on tour. We should do it again, Shuichi."

He placed an envelope in Shuichi's out-stretched hand.

"You might call this a reward. I hope you like it."

"For me?" Inside the envelope he found a ticket for the final Osaka performance and a backstage pass.

"For Yuki?" Shuichi asked.

Tohma nodded. "But *you* have to give it to him. I won't help you with that."

"Thank you!"

Everyone knew Tohma had done nothing but come between the lovers, but Shuichi was too kind to notice. He wiped away his tears and bowed so low his body folded in half like a hairpin.

Then he sprang through the door, shouting, "Yuki!"

Irritated, his lover looked up from where he sat typing on the bed.

This time, he'll accept me. At last! Certain of this, Shuichi leapt toward him, but Yuki dodged him as gracefully as a bullfighter.

"No!" Shuichi wailed, falling forward. His outstretched hand caught his lover's. They tumbled down onto the carpet. In a rare victory for Shuichi, he ended up on top of Yuki, pinning his lover down. "Gotcha!" he giggled happily as he rubbed his cheek against Yuki's chest.

But Yuki's beautiful face just glared back at him, appalled.

"How can you be so cute when you look so angry?" Shuichi cried, wriggling to get a better view of his lover's face.

"Get off," Yuki snapped, both hands gingerly holding up his beloved laptop.

Just then, the computer was snatched away.

Yuki gasped. "Tohma!" He glared as his brother-in-law sailed out of the room, computer in hand. "Wait!"

"Relax. You've got a bed all ready for you." Tohma spun around, grinning. There was an immense, evil power hidden behind his sweet smile.

"Um, this came for you," Seiren said, frills flapping. She placed the silver tray Suguru had delivered on the bedside table. "Have a good time!" She let out a loud giggle then ran out of the room, slamming the door behind her.

"Fall back!" K said, pointing his machine gun, chasing everyone out of the room next door. "Close this room off! Don't let even a single ant get inside!"

Soon the room was sealed off, and all Shuichi could hear was the sound of his own heart beating.

"Yuki, I missed you. So much has happened. But I've got you near me, and that's all I ever need. Right?"

"Stop that." Yuki looked vexed.

"Sorry." *I always say too much. I always make Yuki mad.* Shuichi hung his head, but his shame didn't last for more than a second. He was too close to his lover's beautiful face—the face that made him melt into a warm puddle of goo.

"Oh, Yuki."

"I'm hungry," Yuki said, stalling.

Shuichi was sure he was dreaming. *Did Yuki really say that? Here's my chance to take care of him, but I've got nothing to feed him! Oh, the agony!*

"Wait!" Shuichi said, jumping up. He grabbed the tray that Seiren had delivered. He pulled off the lid, but for some reason, there was only a bar of chocolate inside. "This is all we have. Will it do?"

Yuki nodded. His face always turned angelic at the sight of sweets.

"Aw," Shuichi murmured, overcome. He sat on the bed and started carefully peeling off the foil. Then he was suddenly shoved down.

"Yuki?"

"Too slow, stupid," Yuki snarled, but there was a rare, gentle twinkle in his eyes.

Shuichi wasn't about to let this chance get away. Flat on his back under Yuki, the chocolate bar pressed to his chest, Shuichi tried something he'd wanted to do for a long time.

"Say 'ah'!" Shuichi said. To his surprise, Yuki drew closer, not a single spiteful remark on his lips. Yuki munched away on the chocolate, occasionally licking Shuichi's fingertips.

Shockwaves rolled through Shuichi. The sight and feel of Yuki's tongue on his skin was at once both tender and erotic.

"Ah, careful! Don't get chocolate all over the place," Shuichi said, tenderly wiping off his lover's chin.

"Not enough," Yuki murmured.

"Really? I guess we could . . ." he started to say, but then he realized those sharp eyes were focused on the foil wrapping. "Oh, the chocolate. Sorry. There is no more."

Yuki suddenly lunged toward his neck. "Don't move," the older man ordered quietly.

Shuichi trembled as his lover's skillful lips traced his collarbone, then nipped down his chest. The moist warmth of Yuki's breath made him shiver. He almost cried out with pleasure. "You never could resist a sweet," he whispered.

Little bits of chocolate were scattered down Shuichi's chest. Aside from the elaborate movements of Yuki's tongue, he could feel a large chunk of chocolate sliding down to his belly. Yuki chased it, his fingers brushing against a very sensitive part of Shuichi's body.

Shuichi opened his mouth, ready to scream, but was silenced with a kiss. Their lips locked together, and Yuki kissed him fiercely, as if trying to make up for all the time they had lost.

The sweet taste of chocolate mixed with the slight bitterness of Yuki's cigarettes. Shuichi sighed, unbelievably aroused, and stroked the back of his hand across his lover's cheek.

Suddenly, Yuki ripped Shuichi's clothing off and flung it aside. He pounced, pinning Shuichi's wrists to the bed.

"Yuki?" Shuichi asked breathlessly.

Instead of an answer, Yuki's hands ran roughly but lovingly across Shuichi's skin, mapping him, massaging him, grasping him possessively.

Shuichi's body was hot, feverish. He felt as if he could melt anything that touched him. "Oh!" He bit his knuckles and whimpered.

As he licked a hot trail downward, Yuki's hair brushed lightly across Shuichi's chest, tickling him. Shuichi threaded his fingers in his lover's soft hair and moaned wantonly. He'd never let anyone else hear him like this.

In answer, Yuki cupped him again where he'd never let anyone else touch him.

"Yuki!" he begged, hitching up. *At long last . . .*

He tensed, his entire body trembling under Yuki's expert caresses. His fingernails scraped lightly across the back of Yuki's neck, and the blond redoubled his efforts, kissing even lower.

At the height of his desire, just as Shuichi was about to find sweet release, the powerful urge to sleep overcame him. *No! I can't sleep now . . . I'm about to . . .*

But before he could finish his thought, he lost consciousness.

Shuichi opened his eyes, wrapped in warmth. "Yuki?"

The man he loved was already awake and gazing out of the window. The light of the setting sun highlighted bathed the room in a golden glow.

That looks like dusk! "What time is it?" Shuichi shrieked.

Yuki turned to him, annoyed, and pointed wordlessly at his wristwatch. Less than thirty minutes until the concert began. Shuichi had wanted to make love to Yuki all night long, but instead all he had done was *sleep!*

"Ah! I should have slept properly instead of running all around Osaka checking different hotels!" Shuichi moaned.

"Sounds like your little adventure was all part of Tohma's plan," Yuki muttered angrily.

"I just wanted to be with you!" *And I don't want to leave you now!*

The door suddenly burst open. K stormed in, heavily armed. Shuichi was totally unaware of K's sleep-inducing device and still blamed himself.

"Just a few more minutes, please?" Shuichi pleaded, wringing his fingers together.

"Oh, I get it," K said. "You wanna find out what this magnum tastes like!"

"No!" Shuichi cried.

K dragged Shuichi away at gunpoint.

"So you're going to abandon me for work, are you?" Yuki joked.

Shuichi exploded. "Don't I at least get a goodbye kiss?"

Epilogue

Shuichi's passionate performance that night became something of a legend among Bad Luck fans. His voice was filled with a heightened power that drew the audience to him more than ever before. Several fans fainted from the surges of emotion that his voice inspired.

When Shuichi returned to the waiting room, he got down on his knees and forced the others into silence while waiting for his cell to play that special melody. But he couldn't wait even a minute, and ended up calling Yuki.

Yuki yelled at him, but Shuichi babbled away, undefeated. Even when Yuki hung up and Shuichi was left listening to the dial tone, he couldn't put his phone down.

What drew Shuichi to Yuki was the most powerful thing in the world—love. It was invisible. It was an unstoppable force of nature.

It's Gravitation.

Translator's Notes

pp. 21, 31 *Nozomi* is one of the *shinkansen* routes. The *shinkansen* is the famous bullet train.

pg. 40 Shuichi is mangling proverbs. *Kawaii ko ni ha tabi wo sase yo* translates as "If you love your children, make them travel," but Shuichi gets the wrong *tabi* and changes the verb. The first proverb he actually gets right, except that it doesn't seem to have anything to do with what he's talking about.

pg. 48 Akko is her real name; the pen name "Oh Dear" was a pun on this in Japanese *Akkorya korya*. It's kind of an unusual name, though. Even the "real name" version must be a nickname?

pg. 48 *Enka*: popular singing style, sort of the Japanese answer to crooners. Very melodramatic songs.

pg. 64 Kunoichi: The logo on the memo, possibly Seiren's last name, and also the word for a female ninja. The katakana for *ku* and *no* plus the kanji for *ichi* written on top of each other equal the kanji for *onna* or "woman."

pg. 75 The *inochi* pose—in the shape of the kanji for life, both arms out to the side, downward at 45 degree angles, standing on one leg with the other foot pressed against your knee. Popularized by a famous comedian.

pg. 88 The Dotonbori is actually famous for people jumping into it when sports teams win.

Every year the police warn people not to, since they might drown and the water is really, really, really dirty. But it's less of a river than a canal, and is hardly deep enough for a submarine.

pg. 92 *Toyama no Kin-san* was a long-running samurai drama about a judge who disguises himself as a commoner, then pops his arm out of his kimono to reveal a tattoo on his back proving his true identity. Hence the faux formal language.

pg. 167 *Yakyuuken* literally means "baseball fist." It appears to be a strip version of *junken*, or rock paper scissors.

Fun Facts:

Writer: Jun Lennon

Screenwriter. Tokyo Resident. Born September 23, blood type A. Studied piano in younger days but found the limits of that talent and switched to economics with the intention to become a civil servant. Got involved in the drama club in college, and now mostly writes scripts for TV anime and CD drama.

Artist/Creator: Maki Murakami

Debuted with *Narushisuto no Higeki* (The Narcissist's Tragedy) in the April 1995 issue of *Kimi to Boku*. Currently serializing *Kimi no Unaji ni Kampai!* in Monthly Comic Birz (Gentousha comics) and *Gamers' Heaven* in Monthly Comic Blade (Mag Garden).

DANTE'S
HAVING A
HELL
OF A TIME!

THE NEW MANGA NOVEL FROM TOKYOPOP